also from

aplomb publishing
San Francisco

The Bond that Got Away

The Lost Hitchcocks

Meet the Munsters

Back to the Big Valley

Movie Star & the Mobster

Who Nuked The Duke?

What Ever Happened to Mommie Dearest?

Alfred Hitchcock: The Icon Years

Reel Horror - True Horrors Behind Hollywood's Scary Movies

Curse of the Silver Screen - Tragedy & Disaster Behind the Movies

Master of Disaster - Irwin Allen: The Disaster Years

www.aplombpublishing.com

Goddess
Girl
& the
Next Door

By John William Law

aplomb publishing
San Francisco

Goddess & the Girl Next Door
Published by Aplomb Publishing, San Francisco, California.
Copyright 2019.

978-0-9993069-1-8

1st edition

Manufactured in the United States of America.

Dedicated to fans of Marilyn Monroe and Doris Day.

"All we demanded was

our right to twinkle."

- Marilyn Monroe

"There never was any intent on

my part either in my acting or in

my private life to create any such

thing as an image."

- Doris Day

Table of Contents

Goddess & the Girl Next Door

Acknowledgements

Thank you to David Young for proofreading, Dennis Constan for editing support and Thomas Moulton for assistance with the cover design. Special thanks to the Motion Picture Academy of Arts and Sciences and the Margaret Herrick Library for access to resources that helped make this book possible.

Goddess & the Girl Next Door

Preface

"Being a sex symbol is a heavy load to carry, especially when one is tired, hurt and bewildered."

- Marilyn Monroe

"Why do I always have to be the girl next door? I don't think I ever was."

- Doris Day

Opening Remarks.

Complex Women and the Movie They Both Shared

Having been a fan of Marilyn Monroe's as long as I can remember, I've read many books on the actress and hoped one day to have an opportunity to write about her. I actually did write a book chapter on her work in *The Misfits*. I thought about writing an entire book on the making of her final completed film; but that topic was covered in another book, and I didn't want to cover familiar territory.

The making of her final unfinished film, *Something's Got to Give*, has always intrigued me, but that topic, too, has been covered. In *Marilyn: The Last Take*, Peter Harry Brown and Patte B. Barnham delivered a fascinating and in depth look at the subject.

Doris Day, on the other hand, was a subject with whom I was less familiar. I never considered writing a book on the elusive star; however, over the years I've seen a majority of her films and found her to be a much more complex actress than perhaps she's received credit for. Both Day and Monroe have never been appreciated fully as actresses the way many of their contemporaries have been – in part due to their movie star personas and the types of films in which they starred. With few character-driven films, limited heavy dramatic work, and notoriety for mostly soft, romantic comedies, both actresses had few opportunities to demonstrate their depth. Monroe, the sex symbol, and Day, the comedic actress, failed to earn recognition for their broader talents, even though both showed promise in more serious efforts.

However, the comedies and hits they starred in were often gems due to the skill each brought to the work. Many of these films would have been tossed aside had it not been for their contributions. Today, their work is regarded as timeless and continues to entertain and delight fans. *Gentlemen Prefer Blondes, Pillow Talk, The Seven Year Itch,* and *That Touch of Mink* are regarded as cinematic classics of the 20th Century.

In 2012, upon the 50th anniversary of the death of Monroe, there was a lot of reading to be done about Monroe's life, career and contributions to the world of film – and the star machine that ground up so many celebrities, like Marilyn Monroe, in their prime. I began looking for an idea to look more deeply into the life of the star and happened upon a showing of *Move Over, Darling*.

I knew that the romantic comedy starring Doris Day and James Garner was a reworking of Monroe's uncompleted *Something's Got to Give*, but had never really considered it as anything other than another

Doris Day comedy. It was an era in which she was the reigning queen of family friendly romantic sex comedies. From *Pillow Talk, That Touch of Mink, Send Me No Flowers, Glass Bottom Boat, The Thrill of It All, Lover Come Back* and countless others; *Move Over, Darling* can simply be viewed as another in a long list of Day films that thrilled audiences and made movie studios rich.

Upon closer inspection, *Move Over, Darling* is something deeper – not because the movie itself is rich with hidden meaning or innuendo, but due to the path it took to reaching the big screen and how two women who were in many ways so similar, could be so different when viewed on the silver screen.

The promise of *Something's Got to Give* began in 1962. With the hope for salvaging Twentieth Century Fox, as well as launching of a new kind of Marilyn Monroe, it is a tale for the ages. The movie started off with great promise for the studio, and ended in a crash and burn nightmare, culminating in the shocking death of its star. Like its prescient title, the production is rich with the excesses of stardom and the demands placed on celebrity.

Hope would not be completely lost for Fox, upon the death of its biggest star, when executives decided to try and salvage the movie by renaming it and casting an equally major star. How to take a role designed for Marilyn Monroe and to cast Doris Day in the lead left a few people scratching their heads. Could Day pull it off? Would the movie be a reminder of the death of a legend? How would the public respond, and would the studio survive the investment in both films to recoup its losses?

I hope you find the story as fascinating as I did and come away with new respect for two women who created unique brands of stardom like no other.

- John William Law

one

Goddess & the Girl Next Door

"For me, movie work meant a complete change in my way of living. Where the nightclub singer had gone to bed at two in the morning and awakened at two the next afternoon; the movie actress had to be up at 6:00 a.m., made up and ready by 7:00."

- Doris Day

-

"I'm selfish, impatient and a little insecure. I make mistakes, I am out of control and at times hard to handle. But if you can't handle me at my worst, then you sure as hell don't deserve me at my best."

- Marilyn Monroe

When Marilyn Met Doris.

Very Different Stars, Yet Striking Similarities Between Them

Filmed between September 1 and November 4, 1954, *The Seven Year Itch* was Twentieth Century Fox's latest chance to promote its biggest star, Marilyn Monroe. After toiling away in smaller supporting roles and bit parts, Monroe ignited the screen in *Gentlemen Prefer Blondes*, alongside Jane Russell in 1953, and then again that same year with Betty Grable and Lauren Bacall in *How to Marry a Millionaire*. Fox had created a superstar almost without even trying. In 1955, *The Seven Year Itch*

would put Monroe in the leading lady role all by herself – showing the studio and the public that she could carry a film with little help from co-stars.

In November 1954, upon completion of the film, the studio held a wrap party at Romanoff's restaurant on Rodeo Drive in Beverly Hills, with Monroe feted as a guest of honor. One of the most popular night spots for the rich and famous in Hollywood during the 1950s, Romanoff's was known for its chocolate soufflé and the ability to regularly host a cast of Hollywood stars on any given evening. This was just one of those evenings.

Monroe was running typically late that evening, but she arrived in time to turn heads, wearing a form-fitting strapless, red chiffon gown. Called "radiant" by the press in attendance, the star was thrilled to have finally found acceptance among the Hollywood crowd. She remarked to Hollywood columnist and friend Sidney Skolsky, "I didn't think they'd all show up. Honest."

But they did show up, along with co-star Tom Ewell, producers Darryl Zanuck, Sam Goldwyn, and Jack Warner, and with the film's director, Billy Wilder. A wide array of invited guests, including James Stewart, Humphrey Bogart, Gary Cooper, Susan Hayward, William Holden, Loretta Young, Clifton Webb, Lauren Bacall, Claudette Colbert and Clark Gable, celebrated the night with the cast and crew.

Also in attendance that night was another young actress well on her way toward stardom. Having appeared in a number of films during the early part of the decade, like Marilyn Monroe, Doris Day found her breakthrough role in 1953, in her film *Calamity Jane*.

In many ways there could not be two women so different, yet so similar. Both children of the 1920s, Day and Monroe were a few years apart in age, with Day born in April 1922 and Monroe born in June 1926. While Day hailed from Ohio, Monroe was the product of Hollywood, born in the Los Angeles County Hospital. Both women were remarkably similar physically. At nearly 5'6 inches tall, Monroe was barely an inch shorter than Day's 5'7" inches. While both women's weights would vary between 120 and 130 pounds, they were physically about the same size. Their measurements bore striking similarity as well, with Monroe at 36-24-36 to Day's 36-25-36. Their creamy complexions and blonde hair might have helped them pass for sisters.

Yet, both women had other things in common as well. Both would be avid sports fans, which would lead to reported love affairs with baseball players. They also shared the same favorite singer. Day said it

was through listening to Ella Fitzgerald records that she would improve her singing style. Fitzgerald would credit Monroe for helping expand her career in the 1950s, by helping her play at the Mocambo, one of Hollywood's preeminent nightclubs in the 1950s. "I owe Marilyn Monroe a real debt … she personally called the owner of the Mocambo, and told him she wanted me booked immediately, and if he would do it, she would take a front table every night."

As vivacious and beautiful as both women were, their images in the public eye could not have been more different. Monroe was a sex symbol who made men swoon. Her face, her figure and sexuality were what made her famous – or some might have said infamous.

Doris Day was the picture of innocence. She exuded an image of virtue and wholesomeness that was almost prudish, while Monroe adopted a promiscuous and vivacious persona.

It has been written that men wanted to sleep with Marilyn, but wanted to wake up next to Doris. While Day played virginal, Monroe played naïve. Day's characters could recoil from the shock of sexual innuendo, while Monroe's would simply be unaware. Sex was the required part of the formula, but how their personas engaged with it was where the humor was drawn.

Monroe had to create the sexy persona as much as Day cultivated hers. By turning her hair blonde, having her nose and jaw surgically changed and dressing to accentuate her figure, Marilyn became the part. Day downplayed her sex appeal. It's quite possible their roles could easily have been reversed, with Day undergoing plastic surgery to alter her appearance and taking on a different persona, and Monroe opting for a more girl-next-door appeal.

According to movie box office records, they were both huge box office draws of the 1950s. Day was listed as one of the 10 biggest moneymakers of 1951, 1952 and 1959. Monroe landed on the list in 1953, 1954 and 1956. Susan Hayward was the only other female star to make the same list three times. The Top Ten Money Making Stars Poll was compiled by votes from movie exhibitors across the United States for stars that earned the most revenue in their theaters during the previous year.

When they met that cool November evening in 1954, they exchanged greetings and the usual pleasantries. Doris offered congratulations on her latest success and said it was nice to meet her, but the

women were not destined to become lifelong friends. Marilyn was the center of attention, dressed in a sexy, form fitting red dress. Doris was demure, wearing a high-collar, sleeveless white lace dress. Her hair wasn't elegantly styled, just a simple short bobbed haircut. She wore pearl earrings and a white pearl necklace. While Marilyn danced the night away with Tom Ewell and Clifton Webb, and drank with Clark Gable and Humphrey Bogart, Doris sat quietly at a table off to the side, along with George Burns. She spent a large part of the evening with Charles Vidor, discussing the film they were making at MGM, *Love Me or Leave Me.*

Admiring each other for their talents and ability to succeed in Hollywood, neither had a vast collection of female actresses they called friends. Their paths would crisscross periodically, but take them on separate, but equally successful careers in the coming years. Both released hugely successful films and graced the pages of countless fan magazines. Their careers seemed to bounce off each other with films topping the box office. As *The Seven Year Itch* with Monroe would hit big, Day followed up with *The Man Who Knew Too Much. Bus Stop* starring Monroe would be countered with *The Pajama Game* starring Day.

In 1956, they both sought the same role when Day was interested in heading to London to star in the film version of the play, "The Sleeping Prince." The play starred Laurence Olivier and Vivien Leigh and held promise as a vehicle for Day to show the extent of her talent. However, Marilyn Monroe used her new production company to purchase the rights to the play as a role for herself. She then filmed her version of the story, along with Olivier as her leading man. The resulting film, *Prince and the Showgirl*, was released by Warner Bros. in June 1957. Monroe would earn herself a nomination for Best Actress from the British Film Academy and would win the award for Best Foreign Actress from the Italian Cinema's David di Donatello Awards.

In 1959, Day hit big with *Pillow Talk*, while Monroe topped the box office in *Some Like it Hot*. As the 60s came into view, their careers continued to parallel each other. In 1962, fate and tragedy left one of them dead with the other one picking up where she left off in a movie called *Move Over, Darling*.

Interestingly, by 1962 they both had made the same number of pictures. Had *Something's Got to Give* been completed, it would have been Monroe's 33rd film. For Day, *Move Over, Darling* would mark her 33rd picture.

This is the story of *The Goddess and the Girl Next Door* and the movie they shared.

(Pictured below: The only known photo of Marilyn Monroe and Doris Day. As Marilyn dances with "Seven-Year Itch" costar Tom Ewell, Doris is seen dancing in the background. Photographed by Sam Shaw, Shaw worked on set of "The Seven Year Itch" and attended the wrap party where Doris Day was an invited guest.)

two

Goddess & the Girl Next Door

"When you've been as broke as I've been, you learn to count your change before leaving [the store]."

- Doris Day

-

"No one ever told me I was pretty when I was a little girl. All little girls should be told they're pretty, even if they aren't."

- Marilyn Monroe

Humble Beginnings.

Doris Day and Marilyn Monroe find similar challenges on their way to Hollywood stardom

Doris Mary Ann Kappelhoff was born on April 3, 1922 in Cincinnati, Ohio, the daughter of Alma Sophia and Frederick Wilhelm von Kappelhoff. Her father was a music teacher and choirmaster. While other reports suggest she was been born in 1924, she was the youngest of three siblings, with two older brothers – one, Richard, who died before she was born, and Paul, who was several years her senior. She was named after silent movie actress Doris Kenyon, because her mother was a fan and liked the name.

Born June 1, 1926 as Norma Jeane Mortenson, Marilyn Monroe had been baptized as Norma Jeane Baker in Los Angeles. Her troubled childhood began after her mother Gladys developed psychiatric problems and entered a mental institution when Marilyn was still young. Though she never knew her father, she would often fantasize he was someone

rich and famous. She would claim years later that one of her earliest memories was of her mother trying to smother her in her crib with a pillow. She had a half-sister whom she met only a handful of times.

Growing up in either an orphanage or foster care, Marilyn recalled being raped when she was 11 years old and suffered other sexual assaults and abuse during her teen years. In contrast, Doris started off with a fairly traditional childhood, until her parents separated when she was a young girl.

With her family splitting apart Doris looked for other avenues for happiness and discovered she had a strong interest in dance. In the mid-1930s, Doris formed a dance duo with Jerry Doherty and performed locally in Cincinnati. Her dance career was short-lived when her right leg was crushed in a crash in October 1937. She was the passenger in a car that was struck by a train. Her hopes of a career in dance were gone.

As Doris struggled to recover from her injury, Marilyn faced bleak teen years with life in a series of foster homes. Her looks and figure began to earn her attention and she soon came to the conclusion that her only way out of foster care was to get married. She dropped out of high school and on June 19, 1942, at the age of 16, she wed her boyfriend Jimmy Dougherty. Her new husband, a merchant marine, was sent to the South Pacific, leaving Marilyn once again to fend for herself.

Meanwhile, Doris faced the harsh reality that her dreams of becoming a professional dancer were gone; and she faced a difficult recovery as she learned to walk again. However, hope shined when she discovered her voice while singing along to the radio during her recovery. "During this long, boring period, I used to while away a lot of time listening to the radio, sometimes singing along with the likes of Benny Goodman, Duke Ellington, Tommy Dorsey and Glenn Miller," Day recalled. "But the one radio voice I listened to above others belonged to Ella Fitzgerald. There was a quality to her voice that fascinated me, and I'd sing along with her, trying to catch the subtle ways she shaded her voice, the casual yet clean way she sang the words."

Believing she had potential, her mother signed Doris up for singing lessons. She soon began her professional career as a vocalist. She
sang at a local restaurant and then on a radio program called *Carlin's
Carnival*. During a radio performance she caught the attention of Bar-
ney Rapp, a jazz musician and orchestra leader who was searching for a
female vocalist for his band. Day auditioned along with nearly 200 other
singers. She got the job.

It was while she was singing for Rapp that she changed her stage

surname to Day in 1939. It was also about the time she met trombonist, Al Jorden, whom she married in 1941. They would divorce in 1943, about a year after the birth of their son, Terry.

After Rapp, Doris sang with bandleaders Jimmy James, Bob Crosby, and Les Brown. While working with Brown, she sang her first hit record, "Sentimental Journey." Released in 1945, it became an anthem for American troops in World War II as they looked to return home at the end of the war. By 1946, she had six other Top Ten hits on the *Billboard* chart.

She left Brown's band in August 1946, and began to perform as a solo artist and look to a career in Hollywood. She sang for two years on Bob Hope's weekly radio program and toured the United States.

Meanwhile, Marilyn worked in a munitions factory in Burbank, California. She was discovered by a local photographer and quickly found success as a model. By the time her husband returned from the war in 1946, she had shed Norma Jeane to become Marilyn Monroe. She was already dreaming of a career in the movies.

Monroe divorced Dougherty in 1946 when she signed her first movie contract. She dyed her hair blonde and began cultivating the persona that would maker her famous. To fix a bump in her nose she had rhinoplasty, and would later have a cartilage implant in her chin to change her jawline. The sexy, breathy, voluptuous starlet became the part she would play onscreen and off. She began with minor, forgettable parts until 1950 when a small part in John Huston's crime drama, *The Asphalt Jungle*, got her noticed. A follow-up performance in *All About Eve*, starring Bette Davis, garnered her even more attention, and her star was soon on the rise.

During the same period, Doris was also headed for a career in the movies. She was offered a role in 1948's *Romance on the High Seas* after Betty Hutton dropped out of the film after she became pregnant. In addition to landing her first film role, Doris had her first number one hit recording as a soloist artist with the song "It's Magic."

By 1950, Day was appearing in musicals like *Starlift, The West Point Story, On Moonlight Bay, By the Light of the Silvery Moon, Tea For Two* and *I'll See You in My Dreams.* She married her third husband, Marty Melcher, in April 1951.

In 1953, Doris' film *Calamity Jane* won the Academy Award for Best Original Song with her recording of "Secret Love." The song also became her fourth number one hit. While she longed to be seen as an accomplished actress, her looks and voice were what Hollywood saw in her, and they used her musical talent to attract audiences to her films.

That same year, Marilyn began to break out as well when she

tested her acting skills with *Niagara*. As a young married woman out to kill her husband with help from a lover, she had the chance to show she was more than a pretty face, but Hollywood mostly looked at her figure.

When Marilyn starred opposite Jane Russell, in the 1953 hit musical comedy *Gentlemen Prefer Blondes*, she took Hollywood by storm. The film put Monroe's sexy image to its best use. Soon she was cast in a string of light comedies, including *How to Marry a Millionaire, There's No Business like Show Business* and *The Seven Year Itch*.

In 1954, after filming *Lucky Me* and *Young at Heart*, Doris decided to take more control of her film career and opted not to renew her contract with Warner Bros. Choosing to work under the management of her husband, she focused her career on better roles and fewer musicals. Her 1955 portrayal of singer Ruth Etting in the film *Love Me or Leave Me,* opposite James Cagney, showed she had much more to offer as an actress.

Similarly, Monroe tired of film roles that only accentuated her figure. About the same time Doris was taking the reigns of her career, Marilyn headed to New York City to study acting with plans for better roles and more control over the movies she made. Knowing she was the biggest star at Fox, she held out for a salary increase and more say in her projects. The studio buckled. She also set up her own production company, as did Doris. She returned to audiences in 1956 with *Bus Stop*; acting with Lee Strasberg at the Actors' Studio; and fought Twentieth Century Fox to earn critical acclaim.

Still, Monroe found it hard to escape her sex symbol image. She suffered insecurities in her acting abilities, and Hollywood executives did little to convince her otherwise. As the 50s came to a close, her behavior became even more erratic. Some saw her pre-performance anxieties as bad behavior. Her troubles manifested themselves as perpetual lateness or not showing up at all and often infuriated co-stars and film crews for what they saw as unprofessional behavior. She once joked, "I've been on a calendar, but I've never been on time."

Doris also returned to the screen in 1956 with a big film when Alfred Hitchcock hired her as his leading lady for *The Man Who Knew Too Much*, opposite James Stewart. She sang two songs in the film, one of which, "Que Sera, Sera (Whatever Will Be, Will Be)," won the Academy Award for Best Original Song. In 1956, she also starred opposite Louis Jourdan in the suspense film *Julie*. With Doris playing a stewardess whose life is in danger, the film was a dramatic shift from what audiences had become accustomed to. With no focus on music, the film was unsuccessful. Much like Monroe found it hard to escape the sex symbol image created around her, Day became saddled with the innocent virgin that encompassed her in a host of musicals. "No matter what happens, if I get pushed down, I'm going to come right back up," she remarked.

In 1957, Doris returned to musicals with *The Pajama Game* and then to comedy with Clark Gable for *Teacher's Pet* in 1958. A romantic comedy *The Tunnel of Love* was released also in 1958. *It Happened to Jane*, in 1959, had her co-starring with Jack Lemmon.

In 1959, Monroe found a bit of both worlds, earning acting acclaim and delivering on the sex appeal with the smash hit *Some Like It Hot.* Starring opposite Jack Lemmon and Tony Curtis, Monroe played Sugar, a singer looking to marry a millionaire, while Lemmon and Curtis pretend to be women in an all-female band to hide from mobsters. Her performance earned her a Golden Globe Award as "Best Actress in a Comedy" in 1959.

It was also in 1959 that Doris found her biggest success with *Pillow Talk*, co-starring Rock Hudson. Her comedic performance earned her an Academy Award nomination for Best Actress. As the 1960s dawned she was riding high as one of the biggest box office stars in the business.

For Marilyn, like Doris the 1960s meant she was heading into the latter half of her 30s and knew she'd need to continue to evolve as an actress in order to stay at the top of her game. While Doris had more than looks to see her through her 30s, Marilyn wanted to escape the sex symbol image she'd cultivated. At the same time, she wanted a husband and family, but found domestic peace elusive. Monroe wed baseball superstar Joe DiMaggio in January 1954, but the marriage ended by October of the same year. Though some suggest DiMaggio was her true love, she married a second time in June 1956 to playwright Arthur Miller. That marriage would end in January 1961. Though she longed to have children, she suffered through several miscarriages and one ectopic pregnancy that had to be terminated in 1957.

As the 1960s came into view both women were huge players in Hollywood, but the decade would mean uncertainty, evolution and change.

Goddess & the Girl Next Door

three

"In Hollywood a girl's virtue is much less important than her hairdo."
- Marilyn Monroe

-

"What I like, is to arrive when everything is ready, and then offer suggestions from my own point of view."
- Doris Day

Origins.

From a 1940 Hit Feature Film an Idea of a Remake Is Born

My Favorite Wife became RKO's second-biggest hit of 1940, after Ginger Rogers' *Kitty Foyle*. The script was loosely based on Alfred Lord Tennyson's poem "Enoch Arden" that tells the story of a fisherman presumed lost at sea who returns to find his wife remarried. For the film,

45

the roles were switched, and it's the wife, long thought dead, who returns to the scene after her husband has remarried. Film critic Pauline Kael from *The New Yorker* called *My Favorite Wife* "the most famous and the funniest" modern version of Tennyson's story. It was nominated for three Academy Awards – Best Story, Best Score and Best Art Direction. *My Favorite Wife* became an instant classic.

The film stars Irene Dunne as Ellen Arden, who returns after being shipwrecked on a tropical island for seven years to find that her husband, played by Cary Grant, had declared her legally dead, in order to remarry. As she arrives home, her husband, Nick Arden, has just left for his honeymoon with his new wife. Ellen tracks him down and humor ensues as he tries to find a way to break the news to his second wife that his first wife is still alive.

After a successful pairing in 1937's *The Awful Truth*, Cary Grant and Irene Dunne signed onto *My Favorite Wife* to recapture the box office. The concept worked.

A similar telling of the tale was released in 1940 as *Too Many Husbands* starred Jean Arthur, Fred MacMurray and Melvyn Douglas. In the film, the leading lady loses her husband in a boating accident and remarries, only to find her first husband is still alive. It was then remade again as a musical comedy in 1955 called *Three for the Show* starring Betty Grable, Jack Lemmon and Gower Champion.

The idea was good material for taking three stars and putting them in awkward and humorous situations. So, it's no surprise that in 1961, Fox would begin to think that a remake might again make for good box office. Stories suggest that the film was originally intended as a vehicle for actress Jayne Mansfield. Fox had put Mansfield under contract in the 1950s when Monroe was fighting for creative control. The studio saw her as a possible replacement for Marilyn. However, Mansfield's stardom never reached the peak of Monroe's and by 1961 Fox no longer felt she could sell a major film to moviegoers. One report suggests that the *My Favorite Wife* remake was a planned teaming of Mansfield and Joan Collins, who had both starred in *The Wayward Bus* in 1957, however, Collins has said she was never approached by Fox about the film. It's likely that by the time the screenplay was ready, Fox had replaced Mansfield with Monroe.

Fox had shrewdly tied Monroe up in a contract that, by 1961, had become woefully out of date. The success of *Niagara, Gentlemen Prefer Blondes, How to Marry a Millionaire* and *The Seven Year Itch* earned the studio more than $35 million, putting Monroe's bankability as a star at more than $10 million, considering other hits like *Some Like It Hot* and *Bus Stop*. It would actually be cheaper to use Monroe over casting low-wattage stars like Mansfield and Collins, so Fox brought the concept to Monroe. The risk to Fox was that even though hits like *Some Like it Hot* added value to Monroe's ledger, misses like *The Misfits* and

Let's Make Love added risk.

David Brown was the man who originally brought the idea of recreating *My Favorite Wife* in the form of *Something's Got to Give*. Brown was the head of the studio department working under Darryl Zanuck, until Zanuck was replaced by Peter Levathes. Brown had been managing editor of *Cosmopolitan* magazine in New York until late 1951 when he was asked head of the story department at Fox. During his early Hollywood years, Brown recalled that Marilyn Monroe used to visit his office and sit on his lap, "but that was all, unfortunately."

Brown suggested the idea of a remake starring Monroe to Levathes, who had recently become head of production and he liked the idea. The concept was green-lighted with Brown initially put in charge of the film as producer. However, Brown didn't think he'd remain in charge of such an important film to the studio with his strong ties to former studio head Zanuck. "They would never have turned a Monroe project, especially a big one, over to one of the old crew," recalled Brown.

Brown was right and shortly thereafter he learned that he was being replaced. "Watch out, David, I just saw your script in the hands of Henry Weinstein. It doesn't look good for you buddy," said Darryl Zanuck over the phone to Brown shortly before production of his new film was expected to begin.

Henry Weinstein was a young and upcoming producer at Fox, but not nearly experienced enough for the difficulties of making a Monroe picture. Weinstein had actually produced only one other feature for Fox, *Tender is the Night,* starring Jennifer Jones. The feature hadn't been released yet, but the production had run smoothly.

Weinstein's connection to Monroe wasn't a strong one, but there was one in that he had produced a film version of *A View From The Bridge*, written by Monroe's husband Arthur Miller.

The first version of the new script was drafted by Edmund Hartmann and the film was tentatively named *Do It Again*. Hartmann had held both producing and writing roles dating back to the 1930s. As a screenwriter, Hartmann had crafted more than 60 screenplays by 1960, including features like *The Feminine Touch*, (1941), starring Rosalind Russell and Don Ameche; *Time Out for Rhyth* (1941), starring Rudy Vallee and Ann Miller; and *Variety Girl* (1947), with Bob Hope and Bing Crosby.

The script was revised by Arnold Schulman before it was sent to Monroe. Schulman was the writer behind 1959's *A Hole in the Head*, starring Frank Sinatra, and the 1960 screenplay, *Cimarron*. Monroe got her first look at the script in the latter part of 1961. At first glance, it appeared to be another fluffy comedy that lacked the sort of depth that would appeal to her. While that might have been enough with a hefty paycheck, Fox had her under her old contract. One element that appealed to her was that she would have the opportunity to play a mother of two young children for the first time. She'd also play a more pedestrian housewife, as opposed to the usual sexual bombshells traditionally written around her physical appearance.

In December 1961 Marilyn signed the contract to make *Something's Got to Give*, but it was not without a fight. It wasn't so much that she didn't want to do the film, but rather that her contract with Fox had her earning a mere $100,000 for the feature while costar Dean Martin would walk away with $500,000. While that was difficult enough for her to accept, the fact the Elizabeth Taylor was earning $1 million for *Cleopatra* left Monroe feeling swindled by the studio for which she had earned millions. Since Monroe was contractually obligated to make the Fox film, they threatened her with a decade of legal action if she rejected their project. She reluctantly agreed, knowing once she fulfilled the terms of her contract, she'd be free to negotiate better pay and better features for herself without the shackles of Fox around her feet. Her contract did allow her to request changes to the script, so Nunnally Johnson was asked to polish the story to Monroe's liking and to have a script available by February 1962. Johnson had been behind Monroe's successful 1953 film, *How to Marry a Millionaire*.

After Johnson's version of the script was accepted by Monroe, Walter Bernstein began making changes, because he and the assigned director, George Cukor, wanted the story to more closely resemble the 1940 version. Reportedly after watching Garson Kanin's 1940 directed version of *My Favorite Wife*, Bernstein questioned why Johnson had gone to such great lengths to change the story when the original was already so good. Bernstein was "in favor of restoring as much of the old movie as possible, on the theory that no one had yet managed to improve on it."

Monroe fought against changes to the script and wanted to remain with the Johnson version, which had already had many of her own ideas incorporated into it. Thus began a battle of wills between Monroe, Cukor and Bernstein. Producer Henry Weinstein told Monroe to mark up the changed script with an "X" wherever she saw a line she felt "uncertain of" and a "XX" across any lines she "really disliked." Monroe's found double meaning in his request, seeing somehow that she was being "double-crossed" by the director and producers, as well as Fox executives. It was up to her analyst, Dr. Ralph Greenson, to try to dispel her of the notion.

Monroe did put forth a good faith effort to work with scriptwriter Walter Bernstein, though he found her to be and at times unwilling to accept his ideas, he noted her to be "tentative, apologetic and intransigent" toward him, once giving him the piece of advice, "Remember you've got Marilyn Monroe. You've got to use her."

Marilyn's net worth less than $1 million, far below many of her counterparts. She was eager to complete the terms of her Fox contract and negotiate pay that was more in line with other leading ladies of the day. Doris Day, on the other hand, was reportedly worth as much as $6 million in 1961. Even though both women had considerable worth on paper, in the bank both Monroe and Day had far less, in large part because men in their professional and personal lives took advantage of them. Day had fared well in her last outing on the big screen. *Midnight Lace* did well both critically and financially.

Produced by Ross Hunter, *Midnight Lace* required both a physical and emotional commitment from Day, and it took a toll on her. "I became that woman to the best of my ability. To create the fear, which the character I played had to project, I re-created the fear in myself, which I had once felt in my own life. I relived it. It was painful and upsetting."

By the climax of the film, Day admitted, "I wasn't acting hysterical, I was hysterical, so at the end of the scene I collapsed in a real faint." Production of the film had to be suspended for a few days.

The story surrounds an American heiress who is being terrorized with death threats from a mysterious stranger. The film was nominated for an Academy Award for Best Costume Design.

Day was looking toward her next feature film as well, but Fox never considered offering her a starring role in *Something's Got to Give*. Doris Day wasn't considered a Fox star – Monroe was. It was a Monroe picture – in large part because her contract kept her at the studio on the cheap. While Day, on the other hand, was commanding a far greater salary. Fox was struggling financially for survival and wasn't really ready to pay Doris Day when they had Marilyn Monroe on the hook.

Back in 1956 box office revenue was dropping and attendance at theaters was on the slide. Longtime studio mogul Darryl Zanuck announced his resignation from Fox as head of production. Relocating to Paris, Zanuck set himself up as an independent producer and left Fox to find its own way out of a darkening tunnel. He'd been with the studio since the beginning. It had been a good ride.

In 1932, Zanuck had left Warner Bros. to join Joseph Schenck,

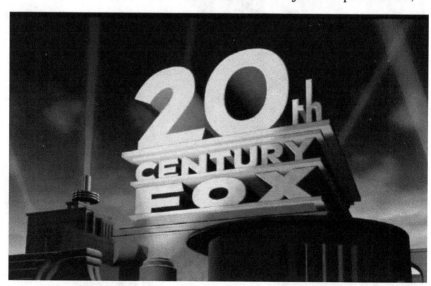

former president of United Artists, to form Twentieth Century Pictures. An independent Hollywood motion picture production company, the film studio negotiated distribution of its pictures through United Artists. To make their films, it leased space from Samuel Goldwyn Studios.

With Schenck taking on the role of President of Twentieth Century, Zanuck became Production Chief. The company got off to a great start. Of their first 18 pictures, only one, *Born to Be Bad*, lost money. In 1934, *The House of Rothschild* was the studio's first film to be nominated for an Academy Award for Best Picture. A year later, *Les Misérables,* the studio's big screen adaptation of Victor Hugo's novel, also was nominated for Best Picture.

However, in late 1934, Zanuck began negotiating with the United Artists board to acquire stock in hopes of becoming a board member. Zanuck became angry when he found out that United Artists co-founder Mary Pickford refused to reward Twentieth Century with company stock. Schenck, who had been a United Artists stockholder for more than a decade, resigned from United Artists and began negotiating with other distributors to replace United Artists. Zanuck sealed a deal with bankrupt Fox Studios in 1935. Twentieth Century Pictures merged with Fox Studios to form Twentieth Century-Fox (the hyphen would remain until 1985).

Schenck took over as Chairman and Chief Executive Officer, while Zanuck became Vice President in Charge of Production. With Zanuck in charge of production, he began signing on a number of up-and-coming young actors like Tyrone Power, Carmen Miranda, Don Ameche, Gene Tierney, Sonja Henie, Betty Grable, Alice Faye, Henry Fonda and seven-year-old Shirley Temple.

Zanuck's production quickly began to show a profit, and it wasn't long before Fox became the third most profitable film studio. During World War II, Zanuck went off to war service for eighteen months, leaving junior partner William Goetz in charge. The War years were big for the box office and profits remained high even in Zanuck's absence.

After Zanuck returned to the studio in 1943, Fox produced a number of serious pictures like *The Razor's Edge, Gentleman's Agreement,* and *The Snake Pit* – along with several adaptations of best-selling books like *Leave Her to Heaven*, and musicals like *State Fair, Carousel, The King and I,* and *South Pacific.*

In 1953, Twentieth Century Fox was forced to sell off its Fox National Theaters and suffered a serious loss. With attendance levels down, Fox gambled on an unproven gimmick by introducing Cinema-Scope. With film studios trying to lure moviegoers with new film processes to offer a unique film viewing experience, like 3-D, Fox mortgaged its studio to buy rights to a French anamorphic projection process that gave an illusion of depth without 3-D glasses. Fox introduced CinemaScope with the release of *The Robe*, and the $4.6 million dollar picture raked in some $17 million in its initial release.

By 1956, the novelty of CinemaScope had begun to wear off, and attendance at theaters began to drop again. The advent of television was beginning to cut deeper into the studio's theatrical plans. Studios like Universal, saw an opportunity to produce television content to fill the void from dropping box office returns, and fared better than studios that continued to focus on the big screen as their main or only source of revenue. Fox was struggling.

After Zanuck's exit, his successor, producer Buddy Adler, died about a year later, forcing Fox President, Spyros Skouras, to crank through a series of production executives, none achieving what Zanuck had.

By 1960, Fox was in trouble. As a publicity gimmick, producer Walter Wanger offered Elizabeth Taylor one million dollars to star in an updated version of *Cleopatra*. The idea for the new version actually began back in 1959 with Joan Collins as the star, but once Taylor accepted, the studio had to up the budget for the remake. Soon costs for *Cleopatra* began to escalate. Tempers flared over the cost overruns, delays to production and scandal surrounding Richard Burton's extramarital affair with his married leading lady. Micro-management by studio executives didn't help, and Fox was close to going under. The studio had two hopes of survival. One was Marilyn Monroe, a commodity they knew well and pinned their hopes on for years. The other would come as a surprise later. It was Doris Day. First, the studio had to deal with getting *Something's Got to Give* made.

In addition to Monroe as star of *Something's Got to Give* and Weinstein as producer, the role of director was crucial to getting the movie completed. While that can be difficult under even the best of circumstances; with a Marilyn Monroe picture, the problems were magnified by the star's tardiness, emotional instability, drug use and general distaste for all things Twentieth Century Fox. Chosen for the task was the incomparable George Cukor.

Cukor was both a surprising and unsurprising choice. Known as the director of "women's pictures," Cukor knew how to both work with leading ladies, and to bring out their best. He pulled out strong performances in even the most lightweight of comedies. *Born Yesterday* with Judy Holliday, *Adam's Rib* with Katharine Hepburn, *A Star is Born* with Judy Garland, and *Heller in Pink Tights* with Sophia Loren were just a few examples of his achievements.

What was surprising about the choice was Cukor's willingness to accept the role. His last film, *Let's Make Love*, left him troubled after having spent months trying to deal with the likes of Marilyn Monroe. However, the star and director were able to bond over one thing they had in common – Fox had them both over a barrel and contractually obligated to make *Something's Got to Give*.

four

"Gratitude is riches. Complaint is poverty."

- Doris Day

-

"Imperfection is beauty, madness is genius and it's better to be absolutely ridiculous than absolutely boring."

- Marilyn Monroe

Let's Make ... Movies.

Marilyn Monroe & Doris Day Light Up the Screen in 1960

In 1960, George Cukor was immersed in an effort to bring *Lady L* to the big screen. Originally intended to star Gina Lollobrigida and Tony Curtis for MGM, the movie was going to be filmed in Hollywood during the summer months of 1960, but floundered when the script went unfinished. MGM spent nearly a million dollars on sets and costumes for the period piece, yet not a minute of footage was captured on film. *Lady L* was put on the shelf to gather dust, until Peter Ustinov took the director's chair, with Sophia Loren and Paul Newman in the starring roles. Completed without Cukor, it would be released in 1965.

Instead of *Lady L* Cukor turned his attention to Twentieth Century Fox for a project that he had been asked to direct called *The Billionaire*. *The Billionaire* was to be a musical comedy starring Marilyn Monroe. Monroe was hot after the smashing success of *Some Like it Hot* and George Cukor had never worked with her before. Her name in the spotlight was sure to bring attention to the film, and Cukor liked the idea of being associated with a Monroe picture. He also had some experience on the musical front.

With 1954's *A Star in Born* behind him, Cukor showed he could shepherd a difficult star like Judy Garland through a hit film. More

Director George Cukor.

recently in 1960, he managed to transform Sophia Loren into a musical star with *Heller in Pink Tights.* Fox felt he was the man for the job for *Let's Make Love,* the renamed version of *The Billionaire,* by the time the script was complete. Cukor liked not only the idea of showcasing Marilyn Monroe, but also the magic of show business theme that ran through the feature.

Born George Dewey Cukor on July 7, 1899, his early career in film kicked into high gear in the early 1930s when RKO's head of production, David O. Selznick, provided him with several major films to direct. *What Price Hollywood?* and *A Bill of Divorcement* in 1932, followed by *Our Betters* and *Little Women* in 1933, put Cukor on the short list of top studio directors. When Selznick headed to MGM in 1933 Cukor followed him shortly after and landed top directing roles for *Dinner at Eight* in 1933 and *David Copperfield* in 1935. By 1936, he was stepping out on his own, hired to direct *Romeo and Juliet* and *Camille* for Irving Thalberg.

By the 1940s, Cukor was known at MGM as the best director for women's pictures, and many of Hollywood's leading ladies enjoyed the chance to work under his direction. His hit list continued with *The Philadelphia Story* in 1940, *Gaslight* in 1944, *Adam's Rib* in 1949, and continued into the 1950s with *Born Yesterday* in 1950, *A Star Is Born* in 1954, *Bhowani Junction* in 1956 and *Les Girls* in 1957.

While Cukor was carving out a name for himself, so was Monroe. In 1955 she entered into a new contract with Twentieth Century Fox, requiring her to star in four films within the next seven years. By 1959 she had completed only one – *Bus Stop* – which was released in 1956. While Monroe shot *Some Like it Hot* in 1958 for United Artists, her husband, Arthur Miller, completed a screenplay called *The Misfits,* which they expected to be Monroe's next film. *Some Like It Hot* was released in March 1959 and was a huge success. Critics praised the film and Marilyn's performance. Hoping to capitalize on this, Fox pressured Marilyn to fulfill the terms of her contract. *The Misfits* was put on hold until Marilyn completed the filming of Fox's next project assigned to her – *The Billionaire.*

The original script for *The Billionaire* was inspired by Academy-Award-winning screenwriter Norman Krasna. Krasna was a playwright, as well as a screenwriter, who also tried his hand at directing. He won the Oscar for Best Screenplay for 1943's *Princess O'Rourke*, a film he also directed. After seeing Burt Lancaster do a dance at a Writers Guild Awards, Krana came up with an idea for a film about a wealthy playboy who learns that a small theater company is putting on a show that makes fun of him. He goes to the theater to confront the creators and becomes enamored with the play's leading lady. When he is mistaken for an actor auditioning for the part of himself in the play, he is cast in the part. In order to get close to the girl of his dreams, he fakes his way through the production while comedy and romance ensue.

Gary Cooper, James Stewart and Gregory Peck were initially suggested for the male lead, while Cyd Charisse was proposed for the

role of the leading lady. Fox managed to get Peck to sign on for the leading man, but instead of Charisse, Fox had another idea in mind – casting Monroe as the lead. She was good box office and a bigger star than Charisse – and Fox had her under contract – the switch made sense.

However, once Monroe accepted her role in the film it was agreed that her part would have to be expanded. Monroe's husband Arthur Miller agreed to do some work on the script to develop his wife's part in the picture. As promising as the idea sounded to Fox, Gregory Peck got wind of the casting changes and put a damper on the proceedings by dropping out of the picture. Peck felt the film's emphasis was shifting to the female lead with Monroe as the star and wasn't interested in playing second fiddle. Rock Hudson, Cary Grant, and Charlton Heston, were approached to take the male lead, but all declined to compete for screen time with Monroe. Eventually, Yves Montand, a lesser-known French actor, accepted the role and production began in early 1960.

Montand started off as a French music-hall singer and began acting in the mid 1940s. With a career solely in French cinema, Fox was banking he would translate well to American audiences and carry his own against Monroe. Her name and body would sell the picture.

Production on the renamed film, now *Let's Make Love,* began in January 1960, and Marilyn wholeheartedly approved of Cukor as her director, calling him, "The best comedy director in the history of Hollywood." In March, Monroe received the Golden Globe for Best Actress in a Musical or Comedy for her performance in *Some Like It Hot.* Shortly after, in April, Montand's wife, Simone Signoret, won the Academy Award for Best Actress for her performance in *Room at the Top.* By the time production on the film concluded that spring, the two couples were close friends, living in adjoining bungalows at the Beverly Hills Hotel.

The film's plot focused on a billionaire named Jean-Marc Clement, played by Montand. After he learns that he is about to be featured as a character in an off-Broadway show poking fun at him, he goes to the theatre to put a stop to the shenanigans. As he arrives, he finds Monroe's character, Amanda Dell, rehearsing an updated version of the Cole Porter song "My Heart Belongs to Daddy" and is mesmerized by her. While there the director spots him and thinks that he is an actor there to audition for the role of the billionaire. Due to the resemblance, he is quickly cast to play himself in the revue show. Clement takes the part, hoping to get closer to Amanda and fakes his way through the play using his mistaken identity to woo his leading lady and possibly to salvage his reputation.

Supporting the leading roles, pop singer Frankie Vaughan has a small part as a singer in the revue, while Milton Berle, Bing Crosby and Gene Kelly appear as themselves in cameo roles helping teach the billionaire how to deliver jokes, to sing and to dance. Tony Randall, Joe Besser, and Wilfrid Hyde-White also have supporting roles.

Filming began under less than spectacular circumstances with Monroe having reservations about the film, but she liked Montand and it helped her to reconsider. The studio, however, had its own reservations about the lead actor. Despite being a successful French actor and singer, Montand did not speak English, forcing him to work extra hard to learn his lines, but, to act the part, he had to work at translating the script to understand the lines he was speaking.

Although Monroe had a reputation of never being on time, reports suggest tardiness was not a big problem during most of filming. Yet, Monroe's relationship with her director did begin to suffer for other reasons. Cukor was mostly troubled by Monroe's constant need for reassurance from her acting coach, deferring to Paula Strasberg after each take, rather than looking to her director for guidance annoyed Cukor. Unable to bar Strasberg from the set, he suffered through it, trying to capture Monroe at her best when Strasberg didn't interfere.

The production suffered another blow when filming was shut down for more than a month after the Screen Actors Guild went on strike. It was then followed by a strike from the Screen Writers Guild. By the time the strikes concluded, the film had lost much of its momentum and everyone associated with it simply wanted it finished. There were reports that Fox executives asked to have some of the scenes be re-filmed, but Cukor ignored the requests and went with the footage he had, rather than try and corral Monroe and Montand back onto the sound stages.

Monroe and Montand reportedly bonded during the filming, and when their spouses departed for other commitments, rumors of an affair between the two stars began. Gossip columns were filled with sightings of the married stars being spotted together. Like Elizabeth Taylor and

Richard Burton, Fox hoped the publicity would drive moviegoers to the theater.

Fox hoped that Monroe's follow up to *Some Like it Hot* would be another smash at the box office. Given the pre-publicity surrounding romance between the stars, the studio was disappointed when the film only pulled in a mere $6.54 million. However, considering the film only cost the studio $3.5 million, due to of the low salary Fox paid Monroe from her outdated contract, the film was actually profitable. It came out on top of the box office in its opening weekend, and would turn out to be the top grossing musical of the year.

Reviews were mixed. *The New York Times* wrote that the film was "slow going," and the directing was criticized, in part "because of poor costume, hair and makeup decisions, and poor directing during the musical numbers."

Some critics felt the film suffered from poor editing, resulting in parts of the film feeling disjointed. *The New York Times* said the only highlight of the film was Milton Berle, who "stole the show," according to the reviewer. *Variety,* on the other hand, said the film "has taken something not too original – the Cinderella theme – and dressed it up like new." The reviewer wrote, "Monroe, of course, is a sheer delight in the tailor-made role of an off-Broadway actress who wants to better herself intellectually (she is going to night school to study geography), but she also has a uniquely talented co-star in Yves Montand. Latter gives a sock performance, full of both heart and humor, as the richest man in the world who wants to find a woman who'll love him for himself alone."

Monroe would later say that the role of Amanda was "the worst in her career." In her opinion, there was "no role ... that you had to wrack your brain ... there was nothing there with the writing," and that it had "been part of an old contract."

As the project concluded, Monroe saw her evenings out on the town with Montand coming to an end. While she enjoyed the champagne and nightlife, some suggest it was mostly just publicity to promote the film's August 1960 release. Shortly before the premiere, Monroe and Montand appeared on the cover of *Life* magazine. Others suggest – even if the affair had started as a publicity stunt – it soon became real, but it ended shortly after the release, as Montand returned to France.

If Marilyn liked the social party life, Doris was quite the opposite. "Party all night? Oh lord! No, no no! I don't even like parties," Day once remarked. Day's friend and costumer Irene Lentz once described an evening with the Melchers as less than extraordinary. "You're invited to dinner at their home, and generally there's another couple there – maybe Audrey Hepburn and Mel Ferrer. There are no cocktails. It's carrot juice at 5:45, dinner at 6, dessert from Doris' soda fountain – where the bar used to be, a movie shown on their living room movie screen at 7, and home to bed by 9."

While Monroe was relieved to have put *Let's Make Love* behind her for Fox, Day had her own career to deal with and a film to promote. Coming in at a budget of $1.775 million, *Please Don't Eat the Daisies* cost MGM nearly $2 million less than Fox's *Let's Make Love*, but the film would outshine the Monroe picture by pulling in more than $7 million.

After its premier in New York City in March 1960, the film would branch out to the international market with more releases in June, August, September and December. While *Let's Make Love* was premiering in the United States in September, Day's *Please Don't Eat the Daisies* was opening in France and Finland.

Please Don't Eat the Daisies follows Professor Lawrence Mackay (David Niven), and his wife Kate (Day), who decide to exit city life with their four small boys to try life in the country. Unable to cope in a small, two-bedroom apartment in New York City, the only house they can afford is a run-down mansion miles from city life.

Coming with trap doors and hidden passageways, they move in to the house and start fixing it up. However, marital woes, threats of infidelity, work, real estate drama and a host of neighbors create humor and fun. It was a wholesome film, fitting perfectly into Day's wheelhouse and what fans expected of her. However, her next film was a bit of a departure for her and for her fans – another thing she and Monroe would have in common.

five

"If you're gonna be two-faced at least make one of them pretty."
- Marilyn Monroe

-

"I want to tell the truth, and maybe that's why they trust me. When I was acting, I believed what I said ... every line."

- Doris Day

Midnight.

Leading Ladies Tackle Drama On and Off the Big Screen

On March 10, 1960, the Hollywood Foreign Press Association held its annual Golden Globe Awards. Vying for the top comedic performance of an actress, Doris Day was a frontrunner for her role in the box office smash, *Pillow Talk*. However, for her performance in *Some Like it*

71

Hot, Marilyn Monroe would walk away with the award. It was the only major acting award Monroe would ever win.

Both actresses were in attendance that night at The Ambassador Hotel's luxurious Coconut Grove nightclub. Located at 3400 Wilshire Boulevard, the hotel was designed by Pasadena architect Myron Hunt and known as a celebrity hangout. Sitting just a few tables away from

each other, the women didn't interact with each other but a drunken Monroe posed alongside Day's *Pillow Talk* co-star, Rock Hudson, with her award. Doris Day didn't walk away empty handed that night. Day and Hudson received the Henrietta Award for World Film Favorites. Day would be also rewarded with an Academy Award nomination as Best Actress for *Pillow Talk*, while Monroe would never receive such an honor.

With Day's last few films establishing her as the premiere comedic leading lady of her time, as an actress, Doris feared being typecast in primarily comedy roles. While the success of her films was without question, and her bankability as a box office star impressive, she was shrewd enough to know she had to show the depth of what she had to offer.

During the winter of 1958, a play called "Matilda Shouted Fire" was garnering attention at a variety of small stages across the United Kingdom. Eventually making its way to London, the play by Janet Green was staged also under the title "Murder, My Sweet Matilda." Universal saw it as an inexpensive little suspense picture and picked up the film rights and renamed the film version *Midnight Lace*, offering Ross Hunter the producer's job.

As a stage play, it was confined to just a few sets when Hunter approached Day and Melcher with the opportunity to star her in the picture. By expanding it beyond the stage, the drama would be a fresh alternative to the comedies Day had been starring in. Day and Hunter worked well together in *Pillow Talk*, and it was agreed the idea was a good one. It would show another side of Doris Day to her fans. She liked the idea, and husband Marty Melcher felt her squeaky-clean reputation would remain in tact.

Hunter originally hoped to lure Laurence Olivier to Universal as Day's husband for the film. Beforehand, Hunter flew to New York to cast several of the supporting roles. While seeing Roddy McDowell and Natasha Perry in the play, "The Fighting Cock," Hunter found the right actors for his parts. He was surprised when he realized the star of the play, Rex Harrison, would be ideal for the role he intended for Olivier. Hunter then managed to lure Myrna Loy to the production as Day's Aunt Bee.

Filming began on March 22, 1960. While the 40-day shoot was well timed, the production was not without its challenges. "I became that woman to the best of my ability," recalled Day. "To create the fear which the character I played had to project, I re-created the fear in myself which I had once felt in my own life. I relived it. It was painful and upsetting."

In the film, Day plays an American heiress named Kit Preston, who is married to Tony, a British businessman, played by Rex Harrison, whose biggest accomplishment was marrying a rich American wife. Kit begins receiving mysterious threats from an unknown voice. He promises to kill her and seems to know her every move. His voice comes on the phone, in the park, and other places and she believes he's watching her. No one else has heard him and some think she may be going crazy. It's suggested that she may be imagining the threats in order to gain the attention of her husband. She enlists a neighbor and her aunt to help her and a collection of possible suspects emerge as the story goes on.

In addition to Day and Harrison, Myrna Loy, Herbert Marshall, Roddy McDowell, John Gavin and John Williams round out the supporting cast. Doris enjoyed working with cast, especially Rex Harrison. She recalled him as a "darling, witty man...with a light sense of humor (that) helped keep my sanity balance throughout the rough part of the picture."

She needed the humor wherever she could get it. Doris spends the bulk of the film being terrorized by an unknown assailant and has to react to a vast array of horrific phone calls and close calls with death. One scene in particular, at the climax of the film, has her escaping on building scaffolding, crossing narrow beams while fraught with emotional turmoil. "I wasn't acting hysterical, I was hysterical; so at the end of the scene, I collapsed in a real faint."

Day had never faced a role that was quite that harrowing from start to finish. The scenes had become so disturbing that, after her collapse, production of *Midnight Lace* was suspended for a few days so Day could recuperate and return with a better state of mind.

One of the highlights of the film were the glamorous clothes she wore, as well as the jewelry, hair and makeup that made her look every bit the movie star she was. Though the film was set in London, the Universal lot would suffice for Day's work. Only some second unit background footage of London was needed to create the scene.

Her wardrobe was provided by Irene Lentz, who was better known simply as Irene on her screen credits. She was a personal favorite for the star. Doris described her costumer as, "one of my dearest friends" and "one of the most talented designers in Hollywood."

With nearly 30 films to her credit, Irene had been around Hollywood since the early 30s and made a name for herself quickly as one of the best costume designers in the business. She left MGM in 1950 to open her own fashion house and put movies behind her. After being away from the industry for nearly ten years, Doris made a personal request for her talents. Universal managed to get Irene to return to the studio to dress Day for *Midnight Lace*. She would earn an Academy Award nomination for the film.

Incidentally, Irene would again work with Day a year later for *Lover Come Back*. However, all was not well in 1962 and Day noticed that Lentz seemed upset and nervous. Lentz confided that she had been in love with actor Gary Cooper, and Cooper's death in 1961 had left her intensely depressed. Three weeks short of her 62nd birthday on November 15, 1962, Irene used an assumed name to rent a room at the Knickerbocker Hotel, where she jumped to her death from her bathroom window. She landed on an extended roof above the lobby.

Lentz left notes for friends and family, including her ailing husband, and residents of the hotel. She apologized for the inconvenience her death would cause. Doris was greatly saddened at the loss of her friend and costume designer and regretted not recognizing the depth of her despair. Had Irene lived, it's likely that Day would have sought her services again for her costumes in *Move Over, Darling.*

    Midnight Lace would be released at the end of 1960 and did well at the box office, but critics found the film un-extraordinary. *Time* magazine called the film "another of those recurrent thrillers (*Sorry, Wrong Number, Gaslight, The Two Mrs. Carrolls, Julie*) in which a dear, sweet,

innocent girl is pursued by a shadowy figure of evil who threatens her with all sorts of insidious molestation . . . Like its predecessors, *Midnight Lace* is not very interesting in itself, but it is uncomfortably fascinating when considered as one of the persistent fantasies of a monogamous society."

Of Day's performance, the *Time* magazine critic wrote, "Doris Day wears a lot of expensive clothes, and in attempting to portray the all-American missus behaves like such a silly, spoiled, hysterical, middle-aged Lolita that many customers may find themselves less in sympathy with her plight than with the villain's murderous intentions."

Variety wrote, "In a Ross Hunter effort the emphasis is on visual satisfaction. The idea seems to be to keep the screen attractively filled. First and foremost, it is mandatory to have a lovely and popular star of Doris Day's caliber. She is to be decked out in an elegant wardrobe and surrounded by expensive sets and tasteful furnishings. This is to be embellished by highly dramatic lighting effects and striking hues, principally in the warmer yellow-brown range of the spectrum. The camera is to be maneuvered, whenever possible, into striking, unusual positions. The effervescent Day sets some sort of record here for frightened gasps. Harrison is capable. Director David Miller adds a few pleasant little humorous touches and generally makes the most of an uninspired yarn."

Doris would be nominated for a Golden Globe Award as Best Actress in a Motion Picture Drama, but would lose the award to Greer Garson in *Sunrise at Campobello*.

While Universal was basking in its good fortune for having Doris Day starring in their new, glossy suspense film, Twentieth Century Fox was turning the screws to lock down Marilyn Monroe to completing the terms of her contract. While Monroe was riding high for her success in *Some Like It Hot,* she was tied to an old contract that didn't offer her the salary a star of her level deserved. However, Fox was heading deep into debt and looking for any way to cut costs or to keep production budgets low. Monroe's contract allowed Fox a chance to cast a major star at a low-budget salary. It was a necessary evil, because another major star was starting to drag the studio into bankruptcy. Elizabeth Taylor had signed on for *Cleopatra*, and her million-dollar salary and costly picture were wreaking havoc on the studio. Ultimately, it would be Doris Day who would help signal a turnaround when she accepted the lead in *Move Over, Darling*.

While Day was preparing for the release of *Midnight Lace*, Monroe was finishing up what would be called her most personal and striking motion picture, John Huston's *The Misfits*.

six

Goddess & the Girl Next Door

"I believe that everything happens for a reason. People change so that you can learn to let go, things go wrong so that you appreciate them when they're right, you believe lies so you eventually learn to trust no one but yourself, and sometimes good things fall apart so better things can fall together."

- Marilyn Monroe

-

Learning a part was like acting out the lyrics of a song.

- Doris Day

Misfits.

1961 Features Offer New Challenges for Marilyn Monroe and Doris Day

In 1940, playwright Arthur Miller had his first play produced. "The Man Who Had All the Luck" won the Theatre Guild's National Award and launched his career. Also that year he married Mary Grace

Slattery and the couple had two children. Several plays, including in 1947's "All My Sons," and 1948's "Death of a Salesman," would earn him Tony Awards. "Death of a Salesman" would also win him a Pulitzer Prize and establish him as one of the leading writers of the 20th Century.

In 1951, Miller met Marilyn Monroe, who was drawn to his talent and mind, and the two had a brief affair. They met first on the lot at Fox where she was filming *As Young as You Feel*, and he was the guest of Elia Kazan. The two then met again a few days later at a party thrown in his honor. They danced and talked quietly into the early hours of the next

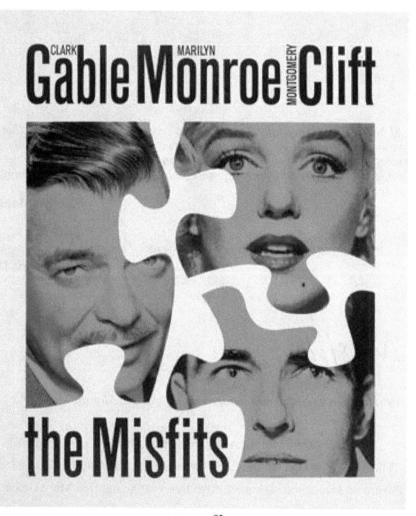

morning. He recalled then discussing the theater and suggested that she go to New York for training as an actor. She was impressed because she felt no one had ever taken her seriously as an actress. People who were around and who heard him, laughed, but he said, 'No, I'm very sincere.'"

"I didn't see him for about four years," Monroe later said. "I used to think he might see me in a movie and I wanted to do my best because he had said he thought I ought to act on the stage." The two reportedly had a brief love affair during his visit to Hollywood and kept in touch. After Monroe's marriage to Joe DiMaggio ended in late 1954, their romance rekindled when Miller decided to leave his wife.

In 1956, when Miller was living in Nevada where he had come to establish residency in order to obtain a divorce, he came across an idea for a fascinating story. Miller had met three cowboys who made their living by hunting wild horses. The story fascinated the playwright and he wanted to put it into words. Since the story didn't fit his usual format – a play, he decided to craft it into a short story that he sold to *Esquire* magazine.

He later adapted the idea into a film. In many ways, the film seemed destined for success. A successful story adapted for the big screen by the talented writer who gave the story life. It was even specifically written for the star actress who played the leading lady. In addition, an Oscar-winning director and a cast of stars that created numerous hits, like *Gone With The Wind, From Here to Eternity, Rear Window* and *The Seven Year Itch*, spelled box office hit.

After Miller and Marilyn Monroe married on July 1, 1956, Miller transformed the short story into a screenplay for his new bride. With the story created as a vehicle starring Monroe, the screenplay found its way into production, but the process took several years, as it usually does in Hollywood. As the years wore on, the marriage between Miller and Monroe began to crumble. Monroe suffered three miscarriages, and each loss, coupled with the pair's well-publicized neuroses, put a definite strain on the marriage. By the time the picture was ready for filming, the marriage was on the rocks.

By July 1960, *The Misfits* was finally set to begin shooting. In addition to Monroe and Miller, the key players included director John Huston and stars Clark Gable, Montgomery Clift, Thelma Ritter and Eli Wallach.

Filming took place in the Nevada desert during a summer of sweltering heat. Temperatures cracking the 100-degree mark made filming almost unbearable as cast and crew struggled to get through each day in their desert surroundings. Monroe was called "radiant" as filming began; but in short time, her absences became all too commonplace and tempers began to flare.

Monroe's unhappiness had her turning to drugs and alcohol to get through the filming. The desert heat, mixed with the Nembutal, vodka

and champagne she was taking made her useless. Filming was often held up while cast and crew waited to see if she'd even show up, or if she did, would she be able to perform? Clark Gable, who was 59 at the time, did most of his own stunts during the filming, because he was bored waiting around for his leading lady to show up. He was unaware what the intense heat and strenuous activity was doing to his health.

Miller had his own troubles with the script, which needed major rewriting, so he distanced himself from his wife in order to get his work done. This only made matters worse, and led to Monroe to suspect that Miller was involved in an affair with Huston's script assistant.

Even so, Monroe was excited to be working with Gable, who was at the end of his career. She saw him as a father figure and in her younger years she even told people she imagined he was her father.

As for Gable, he recognized her talent as an actress, but her problems on the set caused him great discomfort. When filming ended, Gable commented, "What the hell is that girl's problem? Goddamn it, I like her, but she's so damn unprofessional. I damn near went nuts up there in Reno waiting for her to show. Christ, she didn't show up until after lunch some days and then she would blow take after take ... I know she's heavy into booze and pills. Huston told me that. I think there's something wrong with the marriage ... too bad. I like Arthur, but that marriage ain't long for this world. Christ, I'm glad this picture's finished. She damn near gave me a heart attack."

Monroe wasn't the only one with emotional troubles. Montgomery Clift had struggled for years with the difficulty of being a movie star. While *The Misfits* filming went surprisingly well for Clift, it was not without some turmoil for him. In addition to the heat and the trouble with Monroe, Clift had to overcome his fears of dealing with the cast of talent with whom he was working. In addition to Huston's well-known talent for directing, Clift was in awe of the abilities of his costars.

Clift suffered severe anxiety over performing alongside his costars. In one scene, the script had the actor in a telephone booth while the remaining cast – including Monroe, Gable, Eli Wallach and well-known character actress Thelma Ritter sat in a car listening to him speak to his character's mother in a long monologue on a pay phone. Clift recalled the scene as an "audition" in front of "the gods and goddesses of the performing arts." He got the scene in the first take and quickly won over cast and crew.

A major credit for the success of Clift on the picture came from the fact that his role was not a large one. Had the actor been in nearly every scene, like Monroe, his endurance would never have held out for the entire production. Huston once said that he found Clift to be a wonderful actor, but said he was "pretty much shredded" by the time he began to work with him.

Although Clift performed well throughout the production, his addiction to drugs was a well-known secret in Hollywood. However, compared to Monroe, he managed to control it much better while working. Clift also had a more varied drug addiction and used drug cocktails for different effects. Clift's had more to do with his personal demons, while Monroe's sprang from her intense insecurity and professional self-doubt. Clift liked Monroe, and found her to be a kindred spirit. "I have the same problem as Marilyn," he noted after working with the actress. "We attract people the way honey does bees, but generally the wrong kind of people. People want something from us – if only our energy … We need a period of being alone to become ourselves."

For *The Misfits*, Monroe's fear at times was overwhelming. In the first dramatic role she had faced in 11 years, Monroe was portraying what might have been the toughest role of her career – herself. Arthur Miller had written the role particularly for her, even using lines she had spoken to him in real life. This supposedly gave her incredible stage fright that nearly consumed her and made performing nearly impossible.

The effect of the drugs was tremendous. When production began, filming started as early as 10 a.m., but soon the drugs kept Monroe from starting until 1 p.m. Sometimes, it wasn't until 4 p.m. that she actually began working. Director John Huston recalled that Monroe "would come to the set and she'd be in her dressing room, and sometimes we'd wait the whole morning. Occasionally she'd be practically non compos mentis. I remember saying to Miller, 'If she goes on at that rate she's going she'll be in an institution in two or three years, or dead.' It was in the way of being an indictment against Miller, and then I discovered he had no power whatever over her."

If those problems weren't bad enough, things grew worse when forest fires ravaged the Sierras, and massive clouds of black smoke filled the skies. The smoke was so thick that it blocked the sunlight and prevented filming. The electric power also failed, and filming came to an abrupt halt.

No sooner had that situation begun to clear when another problem arose. On August 27, 1960 Monroe had to have her stomach pumped after an overdose. A reporter called the studio that morning to inquire if it were true that Monroe had committed suicide. A member of the studio press office responded, "Why, that's impossible. She has to be on the set by 7:30! Besides, Paula Strasberg would never stand for it."

Monroe was flown to Los Angeles where she spent the next 10 days recovering at Westside Hospital. Production resumed when doctors gave her the okay to return to work.

By mid-September, production was now back in full swing, but worries about the state of the cast and crew continued. Production kept going even as Monroe moved back into her bad drug habits and her marriage to Miller disintegrated. The two rarely spoke to each other on or off the set and there were rumors of an impending divorce.

Location filming finally ended on October 18, 1960 and only a few additional weeks of interior shooting on a Hollywood soundstage remained. When filming finally concluded on November 5, 1960 the production figures put the movie at more than $400,000 over budget. The cast and crew were relieved they had made it through the production. It was one of the toughest productions many of them had faced. But the troubles weren't over.

By 1958, Gable, who had most recently been paired with Doris Day for the film *Teacher's Pet*, was only 59, but had not aged well. Many of his later films, including *Teacher's Pet* and *The Misfits*, were shot in black and white to help hide his aging face and poor physical appearance. He filmed his final scene on November 2, 1960, and told Huston on November 4, "I think this is one of the best things I've ever done." He was going to be a father for the first time and added that, "Now all I want out of life is what Langland [his character in the film] wants – to see that kid of mine born."

A day later Clark Gable suffered a massive heart attack. The strain of the film, the heat, and performing his own stunts were suggested as potential factors in his weakened state. He improved over the next nine days with his wife at his side; but on the 10th day, he suddenly died. Gable himself practically predicted it, knowing how tough the production was.

Joan Crawford told writer Roy Newquist that she had received a phone call from Gable during the production and that he told her, "Joan, this picture couldn't be better named. Miller, Marilyn, Monty Clift – they're all loonies. It's a fucking mess!"

Crawford, who was a lifelong friend of Gable's, said it was the saddest memory she had after hearing of the actor's death. Doris Day recalled her fondness in working with Gable. "I could actually feel the magnetic force of his personality," she said. "He dressed in marvelous tweeds. There was something very affirmative about him, and a directness that suggested great inner strength. He projected utter simplicity. A man who lived on the simple, down-to-earth scale."

Monroe was distraught by the loss of a man she had idolized. On November 11, 1960, it was announced that her marriage to Miller was ending. Less than a week later the death of Gable hit her hard. Having often imagined him as a father figure she was thrilled to finally have had a chance to work with him. Her behavior on the set put a noticeable strain on Gable and the rest of the production, and she was aware of it. Clark Gable's wife Kay was rumored to have blamed Monroe for her husband's death and that only made Monroe feel worse. She was again near suicide said some of those close to her.

As for the film, Huston and Miller continued working on it, but were never completely happy with the results. When the film was released finally, it didn't garner the attention for which everyone had hoped. Many reviewers felt the film never really came together. It is true that both Gable and Monroe were praised for their performances, as were others in the cast, but the film was considered something of a failure at the box office. As the most expensive black and white film ever produced at the time, final production costs put the film at roughly $4 million to produce. Reported box office revenue helped the film recoup just over that, so the film basically broke even, but Twentieth Century Fox President at the time, Spyros Skouras was reported to have said of the film, "Never has so much talent been wasted."

The New York Times wrote of the film, "Characters and theme do not congeal. There is a lot of absorbing detail in it, but it doesn't add up to a point. Mr. Huston's direction is dynamic, inventive and colorful. Mr. Gable is ironically vital. ... But the picture just doesn't come off."

Miller recalled the filming as one of the worst experiences in his life. However, it was during filming that he met Inge Morath, a photographer documenting the making of the movie. The two would begin a relationship, and shortly before the premiere of *The Misfits* in February 1961, Monroe and Miller's divorce became final. Miller married Inge Morath on February 17, 1962. Shortly after, she announced she was pregnant with his child. The first of their two children would be born September 15, 1962. Monroe would naturally have been despondent over the news that Miller was having a child with his new wife. Having long wanted children and a happy marriage, she would have looked at his happiness as a failure, of sorts, for herself.

While Monroe had turned to drama for her next role after the comedic smash in *Some Like it Hot*, Doris Day had gone the opposite route. After tackling the dramatic role in *Midnight Lace*, she would head back to lighter films. For Day, it was re-pairing with Rock Hudson for the comedy *Lover Come Back*. The Eastmancolor romantic comedy was produced and released by Universal in 1961. Directed by Delbert Mann, and with a supporting cast that included Tony Randall, Edie Adams, Ann B. Davis, and Donna Douglas, the film was built was around similar story of the Day and Hudson's first film together, *Pillow Talk*, from 1959. Again, mistaken identity is a familiar theme as advertising agency rivals compete for business and gradually fall in love as Day is tricked into thinking Hudson is someone he is not.

Filled with risqué situations, and innuendo-laced dialogue, Day and Hudson made the most of the comedic yet wholesome moments. She is glamorous in a chic wardrobe designed by her friend Irene, while Hudson packs his own brand of sex appeal, boyishness and overall likable guy persona. However, Day was concerned about the film becoming to overtly sexual. "There was a scene in *Lover Come Back* in which Rock Hudson and I wake up in bed together in a motel, I in pajama tops, he in the bottoms. We have both been put under the spell of intoxicating wafers we had eaten. I felt the scene had a vulgar tone to it as it was originally written," she recalled.

Requesting the scene be modified, Day was happier with the editing. "In the reworking of it, it was established that we have visited a justice of the peace, in our cooky-intoxicated condition, and even though, in the film, Rock is the last man in the world I want to wake up with in a motel bed, and I run out on him, at least we had the blessings of a justice of the peace upon us. This is the film that has that wonderful scene at the end, in which Rock learns I am about to have the baby, rushes to the hospital just as I am being carted into the delivery room and marries me in a cart-side ceremony."

Written by Stanley Shapiro and Paul Henning, *Lover Come Back* would earn an Oscar nomination for Best Screenplay, but wouldn't garner the same attention by critics that *Pillow Talk* did. The film would do quite well at the box office, earning in excess of $8 million.

Day enjoyed making the film, but saw her self becoming cast as a character she was unfamiliar with in real life. "I had become a new kind of sex symbol – the woman men wanted to go to bed with, but not until you married her. Sexy but pure," she said. "One thing I was careful about in those films was to avoid vulgarity, which I truly despise. I liked those scripts about the man-woman game as long as they were done with style and wit and imagination. In my vocabulary, vulgarity begins when imagination succumbs to the explicit."

With both Day and Monroe off working on pictures for other studios, Twentieth Century Fox was embroiled in a colossal mess with another leading lady that was coming close to bankrupting the studio. Elizabeth Taylor was dragging Fox under, and the studio thought Monroe might save the day. In the end, it would actually be Doris Day who would help salvage the studio.

seven

"When I see Liz Taylor with those Harry Winston boulders hanging from her neck I get nauseated. Not figuratively, but nauseated! All I can think of are how many dog shelters those diamonds could buy."
- Doris Day

-

"Give a girl the right shoes and she can conquer the world."
- Marilyn Monroe

Cleopatra Connection.

Elizabeth Taylor Brings Fox To Its Knees. Can Marilyn Monroe or Doris Day Save It?

Director Billy Wilder once described Marilyn Monroe as "Cinderella without the happy ending." Wilder directed the star in 1955's *The Seven Year Itch*, when she was married to baseball star Joe DiMag-

gio, and again in 1959 for *Some Like It Hot*, during her marriage to
playwright Arthur Miller. Wilder said, "Her marriages didn't work out
because Joe DiMaggio found out she was Marilyn Monroe; and Arthur
Miller found out she wasn't Marilyn Monroe."

With the dawn of the 1960s, Monroe's *Cinderella* story was living up to Wilder's predictions. Yet, though her marriage to Arthur Miller
was clearly headed toward divorce, it was her unhappy marriage to
Twentieth Century Fox that was causing her the most anguish.

After *The Seven Year Itch* became a box office smash in the
summer of 1955, Fox knew it was in its best interest to get Monroe under
a long-term contract. As Fox's biggest star of the year, Monroe was the

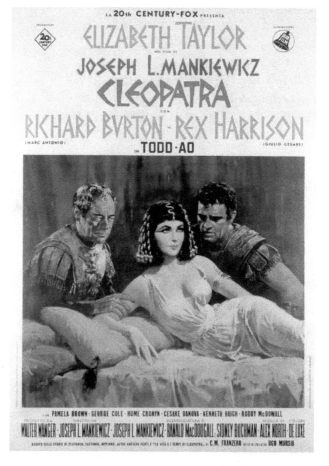

future of the studio. In fact, it was Monroe who had generated the most box-office revenue for the studio over the previous two years. However, Monroe knew she was in a position to renegotiate and made demands, not only for an increase in salary, but also for story, director and cinematographer approval for her films. Fox agreed to her demands and jumped her salary to $100,000 per film, up from her meager contract player salary of $1,250 a week.

Another plus for Marilyn was her ability to make pictures for independent producers and other studios. As long as she made the agreed four pictures for Fox over the course of her contract, she had the freedom to expand her acting capabilities into new directions. Marilyn signed her fourth and final contract with Twentieth Century Fox on December 31, 1955, agreeing to make four films for Fox over a period of seven years. Her films would be joint ventures under her newly formed company, Marilyn Monroe Productions.

However, even though her name was in the producer role, it was Fox that wielded control over the star. They wanted her in pictures that pulled in profits, which meant roles that showed off the assets they thought the public would pay to see – her figure and face in sexual situations. While the roles were merely chances to put her into sexy outfits and compromising positions, Monroe still made the most of it. By 1960, Marilyn was riding high, because that March she was named Best Actress in a Motion Picture – Comedy or Musical, winning the Golden Globe for her performance in *Some Like it Hot*. However, her new clout carried little weight with Fox, only giving them more reason to push to keep her working for them. Now, Fox had an award-winning actress at a bargain basement price.

Monroe's difficulties with Fox during the mid-1950s were well documented. Though it appeared she'd won a victory that gave her newfound control, her own difficulties in completing her films would drag the contract out longer than she or Fox ever expected.

The 1955 contract allowed her more creative control than most studio actors at that time, and stipulated she would appear in only "top-notch productions." Rights to director and cinematographer approval would also be key for her, because it could be the difference between a good film, a great film, or a bad film. She intended to find work that both suited to her and her fans, hoping to avoid the Fox films that only exploited her good looks for big box office. She turned down roles in *Heller in Pink Tights, The Blue Angel,* and *How To Be Very, Very Popular,* because she felt they were inferior.

By 1960 Monroe was well aware that continuing to do superficial films that made her out to be nothing more than a dumb sexy blonde would cheapen her value and limit the longevity of her career. As she aged she knew she needed to expand her roles before the sexy parts dried up and she was left with little with which to follow up.

One part Monroe had her eye was for the title role in Fox's remake of *Cleopatra* and the idea certainly raised some eyebrows. Originally filmed in 1917, starring silent film actress Theda Bara, the movie was remade in 1934 with Claudette Colbert. Fox decided the story was due for a remake, and every leading lady in Hollywood was interested.

Actually, there had been work on a remake, but it wasn't until the head of Fox, Spyros Skouras, saw early scenes of Charlton Heston's epic *Ben Hur* that sold him on the idea of an updated, but lavish *Cleopatra.*

The remake version already in production was only a low-budget film starring Joan Collins as Cleopatra, Peter Finch as Julius Caesar and Stephen Boyd as Mark Antony. The early version was budgeted at a paltry $210,000; and when a larger version was put into production, the cast was altered, and the budget was increased to $5 million.

There were numerous actresses vying for the leading role in the movie. After Joan Collins was cut out of the deal, five leading ladies were in the running for the role – Marilyn, Joanne Woodward, Brigitte Bardot, Gina Lollobrigida and Elizabeth Taylor. Monroe was deemed unlikely to pull off the starring role as a brunette and soon studio heads cut the names down to two – Lollobrigida and Taylor. After viewing the work of both actresses, Skouras selected Gina Lollobrigida.

The studio's only worry was that she was an Italian actress, who, if known at all to American moviegoers, was known more as a bombshell than an actress. Many felt she might not be a big enough name to sell the expensive picture, so Skouras polled U.S. motion picture exhibitors, and they responded overwhelmingly that Taylor was the bigger draw. Taylor got the role. Her salary was approximately $2 million by the time the picture was in theaters. She received $125,000 for the first 16 weeks of filming, $50,000 each week after, and 10 percent of the gross profits, along with $3,000 a week in living expenses. The salary was nearly half the film's initial budget and it was more than Fox could really handle. Both Peter Finch and Stephen Boyd were retained from the earlier version at salaries significantly lower than that of the star.

The first hitch in filming came when Taylor had to film one more role for MGM before she was allowed to tackle the role of *Cleopatra*. The film was *Butterfield 8*, and the production of *Cleopatra* was delayed. Taylor was originally set for the role in early 1959, but filming didn't commence until 1960. By that point, Taylor reportedly called for a new director. Rouben Mamoulian was out and Joseph Mankiewicz was in. Some reports say that Mamoulian resigned from the project rather than deal with Taylor's antics.

Also out were costars Finch and Boyd. Taylor ask that Rex Harrison, Doris' *Midnight Lace* costar, be cast as Caesar and suggested Richard Burton for the role of Mark Antony. Burton had to be bought out of his contract for "Camelot," which was currently on stage, at a cost of $50,000. As it turned out, Fox could have saved the money; because Burton's "Camelot" contract was up in the summer of 1961; and Burton never filmed a scene on *Cleopatra* until the beginning of 1962. However, Fox had no idea of the fate falling on *Cleopatra*.

Location shooting was to take place in Britain. The original film's sets in Hollywood were not expansive enough, and new sets were constructed in London at a cost of $3 million. Production was ready to begin filming when Taylor came down with a cold and became sick and feverish. She reportedly developed meningitis. The crew tried to shoot around her absence, but it was nearly impossible since the script had her in nearly every scene. In addition, the cold weather not only made the actress sick but killed the eight-and-a-half acres of palm trees flown in for shooting, requiring that they be replaced.

In March 1961, Taylor developed an abscessed tooth and then a spinal irritation that kept her from filming. Then, before she could even film one minute of footage, she developed pneumonia and congestion in her lungs that put her near death. When she stopped breathing, an emergency tracheotomy saved her life, but the film would be again delayed. It was decided that Taylor could not film in damp London and production was halted.

Taylor returned to Hollywood to recuperate, and filming was

delayed until the fall of 1961. Location shooting was moved to Rome, a warmer climate for the star to work in. The sets in London were dismantled and sold. At this stage, there was less than eight minutes of footage captured on film, and the budget had topped $8 million. Fox was worrying.

New sets were constructed in Rome to the tune of $5.5 million. The script was tossed out and rewritten, taking additional money out of the growing budget, which was now $15 million. Further escalating costs, Taylor demanded the film be shot in Todd A-O, the widescreen format created by her late husband Mike Todd. This change added another $10 million to the cost of *Cleopatra*. The budget was quickly surpassing $25 million.

When filming finally did begin to move along, other costs came into play as well. Taylor's husband, Eddie Fisher, was signed on as a production assistant, even though there was no idea what he would actually do. He was paid $150,000.

Taylor's other demands during production also escalated costs. Fox supplied her with several Rolls-Royces for transportation. Fox paid her doctor to remain by her side throughout production. There were cooks and butlers, imported china and wine, as well as hairstylists and a secretarial staff. Orders from local grocers were delivered each day to her Rome palace at a cost of some $150 a day. It was reported that her liquor bill during filming topped $500 a week.

Other delays plagued the filming, including strikes from the hairdressers and a group of Italian technicians, and a cast of *Cleopatra*'s handmaidens, who claimed they were being pinched and sexually harassed by male extras. Another story of a cat that gave birth to a litter of kittens inside one of the stage sets reportedly cost the production some $17,000 as the crew dismantled the set, removed the cat and kittens, and rebuilt the set so production could resume.

In 1959, Taylor and Eddie Fisher were very much in love. He had left then wife Debbie Reynolds to comfort Taylor after the death of her husband Mike Todd. Soon, the pair fell in love and married. By the middle of 1961, the marriage was already shaky. Taylor was no longer reeling from the death of her previous husband, and her career and clout in Hollywood were growing each day. She enjoyed the newfound freedom, as well as an Academy Award for Best Actress for *Butterfield 8*. Fisher himself was said to be growing tired of being known as "Mr. Elizabeth Taylor" and even the title didn't get him the work he desired. His work mainly consisted of a supporting role in his wife's last film and a production assistant on her next.

In walked Richard Burton, and Fisher's days were numbered. Burton and Taylor soon began an affair during the filming of *Cleopatra* and their storied relationship has been well chronicled. Richard Burton's marriage also suffered during the filming of *Cleopatra*, eventually ending in divorce.

The Taylor-Burton relationship was a stormy one. During production it heated up and cooled off, leaving cast and crew to wonder if a stormy end to the relationship would cause an immediate and costly end to the film. Publicity managers on the film reported that the romantic relationship developing between the two on the set had the entire cast and crew, except for Taylor and Burton, in knots. Concerns over what the relationship would do to the film's release consumed the studio executives. Fox had created an image of a family-oriented picture studio and the bad publicity of an affair between the stars and their impending divorces could spell box office disaster. The studio tried to keep a lid on the rumors for as long as possible. The cost of the production continued to escalate, adding to the executives' worries. In time, the impact was felt outside the production.

Twentieth Century Fox was near bankruptcy. The cost of *Cleopatra* nearly broke the studio. To pay the production costs, the studio sold off its back lots, mortgaged all its corporate property and cut everywhere it could to make ends meet. By the time filming began in Rome, only one other major Fox film was in production – *Something's Got to Give*.

The cost of *Cleopatra* ripped through the production of *Something's Got to Give*. Location shooting was nixed to save money, even though Monroe's $100,000 salary, due to her old Fox contract, was only one-tenth of Taylor's million-dollar salary. In addition, the fact that she didn't get the lead in *Cleopatra* frustrated Monroe, who was Fox's lead-

ing money-maker, while Taylor was on loan from MGM.

Fox had traveled so deeply into the hole that the only way to redeem itself was to finish the picture and make back the cost. It had hoped that both *Something's Got to Give* and *Cleopatra* would turn out to be big moneymakers, with the inexpensive picture and the costly epic balancing each other out to show the studio a profit. *Something's Got to Give* never made it to theaters, and *Cleopatra* never proved to be the success for which the studio so hoped.

While filming on *Cleopatra* continued, costs moved skyward. More than a million dollars was added to the film when it was shot in chronological order. Actors sat around for weeks collecting salaries between takes that could have been done back to back and were instead placed weeks apart. Production reports showed that Richard Burton worked just five times in the first 17 weeks of the production and actor Carroll O'Conner collected a salary for 14 weeks while waiting to film just two close-ups.

Theft was also a problem on the set. Sets built on overtime gathered dust while waiting to be used or were never used. Swords and other costume items on the set were stolen and then replaced. Massive food bills for catered lunches were handed to the studio for food that had already been purchased. The budget climbed past $30 million to become the costliest movie to date.

In 1962, Darryl Zanuck was brought back to Fox as the company's president to help the studio find a way out of its major financial crisis, replacing Spyros Skouras. Zanuck managed to push the production along to finish in hopes of salvaging the studio.

Final production costs on *Cleopatra* vary. The final tally on the budget was reported to be $38 million, yet some reports suggest that the film actually cost more than $43 million to finish with added editing, marketing and promotional costs. It today's dollars the film is estimated to cost roughly $308 million.

While Taylor made plenty of money off the film, the box office receipts only totaled an estimated $26 million. Therefore, even with the conservative figure the film lost some $12 million.

Even in today's big budget productions, *Cleopatra* is still considered one of the costliest movies ever made, and Fox's hope of making it the greatest epic of all time fell short with mediocre reviews. The off screen publicity of the romance between Taylor and Burton and the stories of the lavish production were the main reasons audiences were drawn to the movie houses to see the film.

Reviews said Taylor's acting was bad and said the film showed the strain under which it was made. The box office receipts would have been considered very strong for any normal picture, but because the film cost so much Fox, never made back the cost of filming.

It would take years for the studio to recover from the cost of Cleopatra. While Monroe wasn't around to deliver *Something's Got to Give,* the studio saw her unfinished film as a movie waiting to happen. They decided with a little adjusting, and a new title, it might make a suitable film starring Hollywood's reigning blonde box office star.

eight

"A wise girl kisses but doesn't love, listens but doesn't believe, and leaves before she is left."

- Marilyn Monroe

-

"When I first started in pictures, I couldn't stand to see myself on the screen ... I'm not pretty enough for pictures."

- Doris Day

The Touch.

Doris Day Brings Humor, Charm & Success to the Universal Lot While Monroe Focuses on The Home Front

Doris Day and Cary Grant didn't know each other well, but they were, in fact, neighbors. In early 1959, both stars had bungalows on the Universal lot. Prior to the takeover by MCA in the early 60s, Universal's studio lot had a comfortable, family atmosphere where stars like Day and Grant enjoyed spending time, even when they were not working. Director Peter Stone, who spent a lot of time on the lot in those days, described the neighborhood of bungalows as, "about 25 charming little duplexes. They were surrounded by lawns, with rabbits running around. Each bungalow had two offices and two different entrances, with secretaries' and writers' rooms. Stars, producers, directors and writers had their own bungalows."

Jack Benny, Rock Hudson, Alfred Hitchcock, Elizabeth Taylor,

Marlon Brando, Audrey Hepburn, Jimmy Stewart, and Tony Curtis had neighboring bungalows, along with Doris and Cary. Stone recalled that, "We all used to sit on the front porch of our bungalows in the afternoon and chat with everybody."

Stone recalled both Day and Grant as being neighborly, but it wouldn't be until a few years later when they would work together.

Hollywood underwent significant changes during the 1950s. A studio system originally designed to churn out films fast and cheap, was finding moviegoers had other options – like television – and they had to try harder. Film studios that once held complete control of the countless contract players and creative talent began to see artists struggle for more control over their livelihoods. For Universal, MCA would later tear down a number of the bungalows and replace them with a big black office tower, and a commissary without windows.

The increased access to television in people's homes meant there was a new business in producing content for the home. However, the bottom line was in keeping the costs down. Hollywood had become much more a business and less a family.

Stars found their options had widened as well, and the fact that their names were on the marquee meant they could have more say in the work with which they associated themselves. They began to demand contracts that offered artistic and financial options, similar to the one Marilyn Monroe signed in 1955. The government also began to force the studios to sell off lucrative movie houses and broke up the monopolistic control to which studios had become accustomed. Times were changing and those that would survive would have to change with the times.

Name directors and established stars, like Marilyn Monroe and Doris Day, grew tired of studios that focused only on profits; so, they began creating their own production companies to make quality films. If the films did well, the stars would earn their fair share of the profits.

During this time, major studios tried to balance themselves on shaky ground by making a handful of good films, while continuing to release low-budget B pictures and delve into TV, intending to make a profit on the cheap films and TV shows, while hopeful that one of the A pictures would hit big.

In 1959, United Artists landed a big hit with *Some Like It Hot*. Billy Wilder's acclaimed comedy went over huge with fans as well as critics. Starring Monroe, Tony Curtis and Jack Lemmon, the film would earn some $25 million in the US alone.

Doris and Rock Hudson hit big with *Pillow Talk*, taking in some $7 million that fall in its North American box office. While distributed by Universal, it was Doris' and Marty Melcher's production house, Arwin Productions, that helped produce the film, earning it hefty cut of the proceeds.

By the dawn of the 1960s, Day was riding high. The reigning number one box office star in 1960, she would hold the title for the better part of the first half of the decade, bringing in more money than any other male or female star in 1960, 1962, 1963 and 1964.

Day's popularity was so high that Universal-International paid the star a whopping $750,000 for a romantic comedy on the heels of smash hits like *Pillow Talk* in 1959, *Please Don't Eat the Daisies* and *Midnight Lace* in 1960, and *Lover Come Back* in 1961. In fact, Day topped her co-star's salary when Cary Grant was fronted $600,000 for his part in the film. However, Grant was wise in negotiating a cut of the profits in the event the film was a hit. A hit it was, marking it the first time one of Grant's films topped $1 million in earnings at a single theater after it opened at Radio City Music Hall in New York.

Day's draw at the box office was so strong that *Variety* reported that when *Lover Come Back* opened in 1961, it took in $440,000 in a single week. "Some idea of how much biz this means is seen in the fact that it is about $200,000 ahead of its nearest rival ... *West Side Story*," said *Variety*. Bosley Crowther wrote in *The New York Times*, "Mr. Hudson and Miss Day are delicious, he in his big sprawling way, and she in her wide-eyed, pert, pugnacious, and eventually melting vein. *Pillow Talk* was but a warm-up for this springy and spirited surprise, which is one of the brightest, most delightful satiric comedies since *It Happened One Night*."

While Doris was occupied with work, Marilyn Monroe was focused on the home front. She'd never owned a home and was busy looking for a place to settle down. Using her analyst, Dr. Ralph Greenson's home as a model of what she wanted, she and her housekeeper Eunice Murray began a lengthy search in 1961. It was late in the year when Monroe and Murray happened upon a modest Spanish hacienda situated behind a tall gate. Some stories suggest that it was Murray who actually found the home.

Eunice Murray was described as a mousy, 60-year-old housekeeper who was selected by Greenson to keep an eye on Marilyn. Marilyn disliked Murray, but hired her at the request of Greenson. Their relationship was called, "cordial but far from close."

In 1961, Marilyn was living in an apartment on North Doheny Drive in Beverly Hills, when Greenson suggested she hire Murray as a housekeeper/companion. Marilyn had fired several nurses and Greenson felt she needed someone to help look after her, helping with her home, the cooking, laundry and other tasks. Murray would have her own bedroom in Marilyn's home on Fifth Helena Drive. She also kept a small apartment, though during her year in Marilyn's employ she seldom used it.

Situated at the end of a quiet cul–de-sac, the house provided much needed privacy. Monroe purchased the property almost immediately for just under $90,000 and had moved in by March of 1962. She mortgaged the home with monthly payments of $320. Financially, she was not as well off as many assumed, considering she was one of Hollywood's biggest stars.

Similarly, Doris Day was in a precarious state financially. After a separation from husband Marty Melcher, Day was looking to divorce until Melcher convinced her that it would ruin her financially. Melcher managed Day's career and saw to it how her money was invested.

When Day learned she would walk away on poor financial footing, she and Melcher agreed to remain married for the sake of their financial house of cards, but little more.

While Cary Grant's base salary for *That Touch of Mink* was below hers, Day and the studio knew having Cary Grant as her co-star was an acting coup for the film. Day generously permitted Grant's name to come before hers as the star of the picture, even though she would be a major reason the film would do so well.

It was out of respect for Grant's distinguished career that she would agree to second billing, even though she was the number one box office star in the world. She had done the same for James Stewart in *The Man Who Knew Too Much* and for Clark Gable in *Teacher's Pet*, though on both occasions her clout in Hollywood wasn't as strong as it was by the early 1960s. For Grant, it was his 69th film, and he was still a major player in Hollywood with recent hits like *North by Northwest* in 1959 and *Operation Petticoat* in 1960. However, Grant was looking beyond his days in Hollywood, thinking about retiring from the movies and focusing on other things.

In the feature, Day plays an unemployed computer operator who is splashed with mud from Grant's car while she's on her way to a job interview. Insulted that he never bothers to stop, she intends to give him a piece of her mind when she's offered the chance to meet the man who nearly ran her down. Upon meeting him, she's swept off her feet by the handsome and successful businessman. Romance and comedy ensue as he proposes a trip to Bermuda. At first, she thinks he's proposing marriage, but later finds that's not quite what he had in mind. Trying to prove to herself, Grant, and her best friend that she's a modern woman, she agrees to the trip, but ends up with a full body rash at the fear of having to sleep with the new man in her life. More hijinks follow when she gets drunk trying to loosen herself up to Grant's advances. Later, she attempts to make him jealous by creating an imaginary love affair with a distasteful man who gives out her unemployment checks. Grant eventually agrees to marry her only to end up with his own nervous rash at the thought of settling down.

Filmed in the early months of 1961, *That Touch of Mink* would be released in June 1962. It was one of Day and Grant's highest grossing films and a huge financial success for Universal, earning more than $17.5 at the box office worldwide with some $8.5 million coming from the United States alone. It was the fourth highest grossing film of 1962. And while the onscreen chemistry between the two stars was evident, Day found Grant a very private co-star. "Of all the people I performed with, I got to know Cary Grant least of all. He was a completely private person, totally reserved, and there was no way into him," Day would say after working with him. "Our relationship on *That Touch of Mink* was amicable but devoid of give-and-take … Not that he wasn't friendly and polite - he certainly was, but distant … very distant. But very professional – maybe the most professional, exacting actor I ever worked with. In the scenes we played, he concerned himself with every little detail – clothes, sets, production values, the works. Cary even got involved in helping to choose the kind of mink I was slated to wear in the film."

The film won a Golden Globe as Best Comedy of the year and ensured Day would remain at the top of the box office.

Doris wouldn't know it at the time, but within a year of *That Touch of Mink's* release, she would be signed up to star in a remake of Cary's film, *My Favorite Wife*.

nine

"A wise girl knows her limits, a smart girl knows that she has none."
- Marilyn Monroe

-

"I was frightened at what that wide screen would do to my face."
- Doris Day

Something's Coming.

George Cukor Is Asked to Bring Life to 'Something's Got to Give'

In 1952, George Cukor was asked by Sid Luft to direct a musical remake of the 1937 film *A Star is Born*. It would star Luft's wife, Judy Garland. Garland, like Marilyn Monroe, could be trouble on the set. Getting a strong performance required a strong and committed director.

119

Cukor had declined to direct the original film, but with this being his first chance to direct a Technicolor feature, as well as his first musical, and to work with Garland, he accepted.

Like *Something's Got to Give*, the filming of *A Star is Born* tested Cukor's stamina. He was forced to deal with an unfinished script that was constantly changing, as well as an unstable leading lady who struggled with chemical and alcohol dependencies. Even on the rare occasions when Garland made it to the set in good form, the challenge was capturing a usable performance.

The film was finally completed at the end of July 1954. It premiered in New York that October to fantastic reviews, and Cukor was credited for having directed another successful women's picture. While he resented being seen as only a director of strong female-driven films, it did make him one of the most marketable directors in Hollywood. In 1962, Cukor was again asked to do the same for Marilyn Monroe in *Something's Got to Give*.

His reputation as a strong woman's director dated back to 1936, when he directed *Camille* for Irving Thalberg. The Oscar-nominated performance by Greta Garbo proved he wasn't just David O. Selznick's boy director, but one who could handle a major female star that could be a challenge.

By the 1940s top actresses began to seek him out, because they knew they'd come off looking their best under his direction. He directed Katharine Hepburn in *The Philadelphia Story* in 1940, *A Woman's Face,* starring Joan Crawford and Greta Garbo's *Two Faced Woman* in 1941, Ingrid Bergman in *Gaslight* in 1944, and Hepburn again in *Adam's Rib* in 1949 were some of his successes. The trend continued in the 1950s and beyond with *Born Yesterday, A Star Is Born, Bhowani Junction*, and *Les Girls.*

He was hired to direct *Gone with the Wind* by Selznick in 1936 and spent a remarkable amount of time coaching both Vivien Leigh and Olivia de Havilland to be southern belles before production began. However, before principal photography could start, Selznick replaced Cukor with Victor Fleming, because he felt Cukor's slow pace might derail the complicated filming. The friendship between Selznick and Cukor nearly came to an end, but losing the film actually freed Cukor up to direct *The Women* in 1939. It was notable for its all-female cast, and would help cement Cukor as one of the best directors a leading lady could ask for.

By the early 60s though, some of his luster had worn off. Neither of his last two films, *Heller in Pink Tights* or *Let's Make Love*, was a box office hit. Some were surprised at his willingness to reteam with Monroe for *Something's Got to Give*, after the difficulties of *Let's Make Love*. However, Cukor actually liked Monroe, even though he found her erratic and difficult on the set. Some suggest that Cukor hoped if he

could pull out a strong Monroe performance and create a box office hit, it would be the win he needed to lift what had become a sagging career. However, more than that, Fox had signed Cukor to a two-picture deal, and after *Let's Make Love*, the studio had him on the hook for one more film. They assigned him to direct *Something's Got to Give* after Monroe asked the studio to select another director, because she didn't want Frank Tashlin, who'd had recent successes with *The Girl Can't Help It* and *Will Success Spoil Rock Hunter?*, starring Jayne Mansfield, and *The Geisha Boy* and *Cinderfella*, starring Jerry Lewis.

As for Monroe, she could have used a hit too. While *Some Like It Hot* had been a smash, the new decade left some questioning if she were on the decline. Both *The Misfits* and *Let's Make Love* failed to live up to expectations. While she was not entirely responsible for the lackluster box office of the films, her erratic behavior on the set was well known and any failure was always partly attributed to the trouble she could cause for the director, the crew and her fellow cast members. However, with age Monroe began to mature, and some hoped she would settle down and become more focused on her profession.

By 1962, Marilyn had lived at 42 different homes, apartments or hotels until finally settling into her last residence, a small home at 12305 Fifth Helena Drive in Brentwood California. Complete with a pool out back, flanked by several large palm trees, it was the only house she ever owned, having purchased it in January 1962. Silent film actor, Dick Hunter previously owned the home.

The single story home, covered in white stucco with a red tile roof, had three bedrooms and two bathrooms. The master bedroom was quiet and would provide Monroe the privacy she desired, and a second bedroom would be for her housekeeper. The third acted as a "telephone room" and guest room. Out the back of the house was a "not-quite-kidney-shaped" swimming pool in the backyard along with a detached guesthouse that offered privacy to any guest she might ask to stay with her. Monroe reportedly never used the pool.

Her house could be best described as a Spanish-style bungalow with a clay-tiled roof. Built in 1929, the house was shielded on one side by a wall and several Eucalyptus trees. Monroe installed a large antique

wooden gate at the driveway entrance for added privacy. Many say she fell in love with the house the instant she saw it, and said it was the only space she ever felt safe. "I want a hideaway, a place where I can go and live a completely private life."

She began moving into the home in February and took a trip to Mexico where she picked up some tin masks and an Aztec calendar for the home. In between pictures, she had the time to settle in and get the home set up the way she wanted, for herself and her sometimes live-in housekeeper, Eunice Murray. For privacy, she hung sheets over the windows before the drapes arrived. By late March, work was still being done. When the plumbing was being worked on, Monroe actually had to leave the house in the morning and drive over to Ralph Greenson's to wash her hair and to return home to get ready for the rest of her day.

Before heading to Mexico, Marilyn had a brief trip to New York. She took her new secretary, Cherie Redmond, along for business and immediately formed a strong opinion on the woman. "She must never be allowed in my home," Marilyn told her housekeeper Eunice Murray, while in Mexico City.

Marilyn and her secretary were in New York on business that included some work with Twentieth Century Fox. The pair stayed together in Marilyn's New York apartment, but a clash in personalities showed the two would never be friends. "Mr. Rudin says she's a good secretary, and I guess she is," Marilyn told Murray. "But she can't be one of my close friends."

Marilyn's reaction had been adverse from the moment she heard her name from the attorney. "Cherie?" Marilyn had said on the phone. "Oh, no, not another Cherie!" [It had been the name of her character in the movie, *Bus Stop*.] "Couldn't she have another name?" Marilyn asked. Redmond was paid $250 per week to handle Monroe's business affairs, but Marilyn made it clear to Murray, "She is not one of the people who will be invited to my home."

If Marilyn had to sign documents or checks, she arranged to

have Murray meet her at the gate of Marilyn's home, and Redmond had to write down anything she needed from Monroe to avoid interaction. "I don't want her advice about anything but business matters," she told the housekeeper. "Besides," Marilyn added, joking, "She drank up the last of my Dom Perignon."

Marilyn's Brentwood home was about 25 minutes down Sunset Boulevard from Doris Day's larger Beverly Hills home. Day and Melcher bought their five-bedroom home on Crescent Drive in the 1950s. The 4,300 square foot house was built in 1922 and was much larger than Monroe's home.

Something's Got to Give went into pre-production in January 1962. The lot at Twentieth Century Fox was virtually empty. Except for this one production, no other work was going on at the Hollywood studio. In fact, the only other production underway was the troubled *Cleopatra*, off shooting in Europe with Elizabeth Taylor and Richard Burton and raking up debt the studio couldn't afford to pay. It was a sad state of affairs for the studio that once held the title as the biggest of them all in Hollywood.

Only a decade earlier, in 1953, Fox's *The Robe* was the number one picture of the year. Pulling in $17.5 million in its initial release, it came in $5 million ahead of its nearest competitor, *From Here to Eternity*. The widescreen epic was so massive that Darryl Zanuck announced that all Fox pictures going forward would be made using CinemaScope. That same year, Marilyn Monroe's *How to Marry a Millionaire* would also be released with the treatment, pulling in $7.5 million and making it the fourth biggest hit of the year, ensuring Fox was financially sound. Soon, other studios like Warner Bros., MGM, Universal, and Columbia Pictures would adopt the process, adding more revenue to the Fox coffers. Doris Day also scored big in 1953, starring in *Calamity Jane*. While not as high profile as what was going on at Fox, Day's Warner Bros. picture established her as a woman clearly capable of pulling off a strong performance and selling it to a willing public.

Though CinemaScope caused a brief up-tick in audiences as it competed with the new television sets appearing in living rooms across the country, by 1956 numbers once again began to slide. Fox had spent a large amount of money helping movie houses upgrade their equipment to use the CinemaScope treatment. Fox needed strong hits to stay viable. *The King and I* was the only big Fox hit that year, far behind Paramount's *The Ten Commandments*. Marilyn Monroe again helped keep Fox profitable with her hit *Bus Stop*, which came in with nearly $7.3 million, well above its $2.2 million budget – half the cost of *The King and I*. Doris Day would score big with Hitchcock's *The Man Who Knew Too Much* in 1956, along with a small picture, *Julie*, where she played a stewardess being terrorized by Louis Jordan.

Darryl Zanuck had announced his resignation as head of production that year, and his successor, Buddy Adler, died a year later, leaving Fox President Spyros Skouras to run through a series of production heads, but not enough hits. By 1962, Fox was in trouble. *Cleopatra* was draining the company of every dime it had. The remaking the 1940s hit, *My Favorite Wife* was actually rushed into production. It was a Hail Mary pass, hoping to bring in enough cash to keep Fox afloat. Retitled *Something's Got To Give*, it would star Marilyn.

The studio could keep costs down by casting Monroe, with her old contact, and suggested Doris Day's leading man on *The Thrill of it All*, James Garner, as her leading man. Monroe, on the other hand, wanted a more bankable leading man and requested Dean Martin. Since she had approval of her costar, Garner was out and Fox gave in. Other supporting roles included Cyd Charisse as wife number two, Bianca Arden, and Tom Tryon as Monroe's lost-at-sea companion, Stephen Burkett. Cameo appearances from familiar faces and popular comedians, Wally Cox, Phil Silvers, and John McGiver would also be highlights of the picture. Monroe's mother-in-law for the film was expected to be a familiar face when Thelma Ritter's name was mentioned for a part. Ritter and Monroe had last worked together in *The Misfits*. Ritter, in fact, would have been the only original cast member to appear in the reworked version, *Move Over, Darling*, though she never actually filmed scenes for *Something's Got to Give*. Garner would get his chance to play leading man in the remake.

Cukor liked his leading lady, but found Monroe difficult to deal with, in part due to her poor work habits and frequent absences from the set. "I found her extremely intelligent – inarticulate, but extremely intelligent – and driven," Cukor said of working with Marilyn. "In certain ways she was very shrewd. I once heard her talk in her ordinary voice, which was quite unattractive. So, she invented this appealing baby voice. Also, you very seldom saw her with her mouth closed, because when it was closed she had a very determined chin, almost a different face. The face moved in a wonderful way. It was a wonderful movie face.

However, Cukor's main pain point in dealing with Monroe, was the constant hovering presence of her acting coach, Paula Strasberg. Having suffered through *Let's Make Love*, Cukor knew too well that Strasberg was Monroe's "acting crutch." One he would have trouble getting around.

Born Pearl Miller, Paula Strasberg was a second rate actress that failed to connect with audiences. She had made her stage debut on Broadway in 1927 in a play called "The Cradle Song." She would appear in some 20 plays over then next 20 years. Her first marriage to Harry Stein would end after six years in 1935. She married Lee Strasberg several days after the divorce of her first marriage became final. While she had no children with Stein, she and Lee Strasberg would have two children, Susan and John.

Lee Strasberg was born in Poland and, as a child, came to the United States, where he had a brief acting career. In 1931, he helped found the Group Theatre in New York. Initially focusing on directing plays, he found his talent lay in training young actors. Through the Actors Studio, he focused on "method" acting, a process brought to America by Konstantin Stanislavski. His work quickly gained a following in the 1950s when actors like James Dean, Anne Bancroft, Kim Hunter, Julie Harris, Paul Newman and Rod Steiger attended his classes.

Marilyn Monroe found Lee Strasberg in New York around 1955 as she looked to become a better actress. Attending classes at the Actors Studio, Monroe would often take notes of breakthrough moments she discovered while there. The work made her question herself, but also strive to be better. She once wrote, "Why did it mean so much to me?... Strasberg makes me feel badly [that I was acting out of "fear"]... You must start to do things out of strength... by not looking for strength, but only looking and seeking technical ways and means."

Strasberg's work with Monroe offered him even more fame than he had expected, and the opportunity to shape this star into a formidable actress was a challenge he fully accepted. He soon welcomed Monroe into his home and his family. Monroe quickly became attached to his wife and children. When she returned to Hollywood to work, Paula Strasberg came with her, offering her moral support and advice on her performance. Monroe became so dependent on Strasberg before her scenes that she looked to her for guidance, rather than to her director.

This created tension between the star and her directors, as well as with others in the cast and the crew during her last few films. Many feared the trouble would continue for *Something's Got to Give*, but there was little they could do about it.

Something's Got to Give was on the calendar for spring 1962, in part because Dean Martin was wrapped up with another film and an equally challenging leading lady – Lana Turner. Many leading ladies of Hollywood had a thing for Dean Martin. Marilyn Monroe loved a guy that could make her laugh, as did many other blonde beauties like Doris Day, Jayne Mansfield and Lana Turner. Dean Martin's tall, dark and handsome looks didn't hurt either. Before Dean could tackle *Something's Got to Give*, he had another project in his sights called *Who's Got the Action*. His costar was Lana Turner, a femme fatal with whom Dean was well acquainted.

In the late 1940s, Lana and Dean traveled in the same circle. Ciro's was a popular hangout for the young Hollywood set, and both Lana and Dean were known to frequent the locale, as was Monroe. One of the men who knew best was Herman Hover, proprietor of Ciro's.

Located on Sunset Boulevard on the Sunset Strip, Ciro's opened in 1940 under the ownership of William Wilkerson, but Hover took over the hot spot in 1942 and ran it as the hottest club in West Hollywood until it closed its doors in 1957. "Ciro's did terrific," Hover said. "Everyone thought Howard Hughes was backing me, but there were no partners."

Hover said back in the early days after the club closed there was always a handful of celebrities and their pals on hand. Doris Day and Marty Melcher frequented Ciros in the 1950s, and Marilyn Monroe was pictured there on numerous occasions before the restaurant closed.

Based on the 1960 novel, *Four Horse Players Are Missing* by Alexander Rose, in *Who's Got the Action?* Dean plays a husband with a gambling addiction, while his wife finds herself wrapped up in trouble when she pretends to be his bookie. Directed by Daniel Mann, it was co-produced through Dean's own production company – Claude Productions – and Paramount Pictures. Production began in January 1962 and it would take several months before Martin was available to head over to Fox for *Something's Got to Give*.

In the meantime, before filming was set to begin in April, Fox focused on building the sets for *Something's Got to Give*. The main soundstage, where much of the story was to take place, featured a house that resembled George Cukor's own home.

Cukor's own home became an inspiration for the set from the director, who had spent years turning his house into a showplace for the Hollywood elite. Cukor bought the house around 1934, intent on a major remodel. Nestled in the Hollywood Hills above the Sunset Strip, Cukor worked with architect Michael Delina to rebuild the small house into something grander. A large terrace garden with Italian statues was added and lit by tinted, concealed lighting. Ivy-covered walls surrounded the grounds for added privacy. The swimming pool in back was added for entertaining in the southern California sun. Cukor's friend, actor and designer William Haines was hired to decorate the interior. Cukor wanted the furnishings to highlight his collection of art, which include works by Picasso, Toulouse-Lautrec, Renoir and Henry Moore, as well as a bronze sculpture by Rodin.

The replica of Cukor's home built on the Fox lot became the main set for the home in the film. Included was an exact copy of his swimming pool, and a scene was written into the story that would feature Monroe going for a sexy nighttime swim. The scene would be nixed in the *Move Over, Darling* version, with a family swim sequence in the daytime making the most use of the pool.

Another set, featuring a tropical island for an elaborate dream sequence, was added, but would the scene would never be filmed. Special lighting was built above the soundstages to soften Monroe's lines as she aged, hoping to erase years and to keep her looking her best. Doris Day would make use of the lighting set-up herself a year later.

On April 10, 1962, screen tests of Monroe, in character, were scheduled to test the costumes and hairstyles to be used in the picture.

After roughly 16 months away from a movie set, Marilyn Monroe was up at 4 a.m., preparing herself for a busy day, and by roughly 8 a.m. a royal-blue limousine with the gold leaf lettering on the door that read "Twentieth Century-Fox" arrived outside her home to drive to the studio. Arriving at 9 a.m. at her small bungalow, she would prepare for a lengthy series of shots that each required a costume change, make-up and hairstyles to offer movie audiences a new side to Marilyn Monroe – as wife and mother.

Six hours of filming her in mature yet elegant costumes, with featuring hairstyles that softened an aging yet beautiful Marilyn Monroe delivered a new goddess. Hours of additional time to get her ready for each test was required, with the plan to reintroduce her with a character that wore department store dresses and casual hairstyles. Monroe wasn't taking any risks, asking renowned designer Jean Louis to design the clothes for her mature new image. Hairstylist Sidney Guilaroff was asked to provide six classy and softer hairstyles. Monroe's make-up artist Whitey Snyder knew her better than most and could bring out the best in her in front of the camera. For her "less glamorous" look, he would mix Max Factor's sun tan base makeup with a half-cup of ivory coloring and an "eye-dropper" of Clown White color. This combination matched the star's skin tone perfectly and wasn't used just for her face, but for full body makeup in the swimming sequences, and other shots where Monroe was wearing little. While the idea was to introduce a more mature Marilyn Monroe to audiences, fans would expect some skin and sex appeal; so the script would feature enough of both.

Monroe tested several dresses, coats and hats that day, as well as a sexy light-green bikini. The bathing suit was specially designed to show off Monroe's new, slim figure while still hiding her belly button, one of the studio's censorship requirements.

The crew whistled and cheered as she walked onto the closed set. "The change in her was breathtaking," commented designer Jean Louis. "It was made even more startling, because Marilyn had just lost twenty-five pounds. She had never been so slim and glowing."

While the day was a success for the star, it was not without incident. Monroe faced the long and grueling day with grace, making all the costume changes and filming on schedule and to the camera's demands. However, director George Cukor, wasn't the man behind the camera lens filming it all. Cukor sent a memo in which the director stated that he "politely and regretfully bowed out of the tests." The crew surmised that Cukor was busy casting the child actors, but the memo simply stated "pressing production business."

Some felt his absence was an insult to the star and started the picture off on a very poor note. It was a long-standing tradition that the director be there for his leading lady's tests, Cukor and Monroe had not ended on the best of terms after completing *Let's Make Love*; so, many were surprised Cukor had even agreed to work with her at all.

Once actual filming began, things didn't look any better. Cukor and Monroe suffered with one another, and Monroe soon began finding it impossible to get to the set at all. The pace of filming became troublesome with Cukor struggling with both the script and the star. Soon, Fox was putting pressure on everyone to speed things up. Instead, things were about to get a lot worse.

ten

"Some of the downbeat pictures, in my opinion, should never be made at all. Most of them are made for personal satisfaction, to impress other actors who say 'Oh, God! What a shot, what camera work!' But the average person in the audience, who bought his ticket to be entertained, doesn't see that at all. He comes out depressed."

- Doris Day

"The trouble with censors is that they worry if a girl has cleavage. They ought to worry if she hasn't any."

- Marilyn Monroe

Pressure.

The Studio Feels the Pressure As Problems Mount

After Marilyn Monroe's successful hair and costume screen tests, Fox felt they had crossed a hurdle and could move forward to aggressively get *Something's Got to Give* in the film can. However, several weeks of script rewrites were needed, slowing down the production. It was a situation Fox could not afford.

Back in 1946, when Marilyn Monroe first set foot on its sound stages, Fox was a giant. Grossing more than $185 million that year, it out-grossed its nearest rival, Paramount by some $25 million. Not just financially, but also in physical size, Fox was a behemoth with 16 sound stages covering more than 300 acres of prime California real estate. By the end of the 1940s it employed some 4,000 people. However, times had changed, and by the time *Something's Got to Give* went before the cameras, it was nearly bankrupt.

By 1962, the studio no longer had the cash on hand to get productions underway and had begun selling off every valuable asset it had to keep from going under. As sets for *Something's Got to Give* were being built on the only sound stage left in use, the studio had fewer than 900 employees on the lot. Even the land below the film's production had been sold to the Aluminum Corporation of America, so the studio had to lease back the space back temporarily. As Monroe arrived on the Fox lot for work, Aluminum Corporation of America construction crews were already at work dismantling the property, with plans to put up a corporate office complex and residential condos.

Between 1959 and 1962 Fox lost $61 million. While MGM came out with a huge hit in *Ben Hur*, United Artists hit it big with Monroe's *Some Like It Hot*, and Universal was on the table with hits like *Spartacus, Operation Petticoat* and Doris Day's *Pillow Talk*, Fox had a dismal five years with no hits to speak of. What was worse for the studio was its dependence on hits. While most other studios, by 1960, had been merged or taken over by conglomerates, with divested entertainment interests in television, actor representation, and other entertainment-related endeavors, Fox's income was almost wholly dependent on income from feature-film productions. When its films simply cost more than the back office recouped at the theater the studio saw red, lots of red.

In 1961 alone, Fox spent nearly $21 million trying to keep *Cleopatra* from sinking under the weight of itself. The studio reportedly lost $20 million that year and pinned its hopes on finishing the costly film, while keeping *Something's Got to Give* under budget. With Taylor

and Monroe as stars, it felt that both films would reap rewards at the box office and return cash to the struggling front office.

As the studio geared up to start production on the Monroe picture, the sets were completed, a production schedule put into place, and the costumes, hair and make-up issues addressed; a smooth start would get the film off on a good note.

On April 13, Monroe agreed to attend a script conference with Cukor and screenwriter Walter Bernstein, art director and associate producer Gene Allen, and producer Henry Weinstein. While the meeting was scheduled for 10 a.m., Monroe strolled in to the meeting at noon, offering apologies for her tardiness. However, it was little surprise, as Monroe was never on time for anything. She'd been late for her first screen test, as well as the premiere of *Gentlemen Prefer Blondes*. She even once admitted she was, "psychologically incapable of being on time."

At the meeting, Monroe rolled through a series of "suggestions" to the script while the men heard her out. She then announced she was headed to New York to visit her acting coach, Lee Strasberg and his wife, Paula. Going over her impending role, she hoped the team from the Actors Studio would help her with the motivation and depth she wanted. "I've got to oil the old pipes … to tune up my technique," she told Henry Weinstein.

Playing a mother of two young children was a new experience for Monroe. Without children of her own, she saw this as an opportunity to look behind the persona that Hollywood had built around her and to show a side of her that could serve her career well in the years ahead.

Since Monroe's "suggestions" required rewrites, Cukor and Bernstein worked on the script, while Cukor also still had the key task of casting Monroe's screen children and other small parts. The production was delayed about three weeks, with Monroe remaining in New York during the pre-production work. Some reports suggest that her visit with the Strasbergs was, in part, a cover for a romantic liaison with President

John F. Kennedy, with whom Monroe was rumored to be having an affair. By the end of her visit, she developed a cold.

When Monroe returned to Hollywood on April 19, she was quite ill. She awoke at 3:30 a.m. on April 20 suffering chills and fever. Her bed was soaked from perspiration as she shivered beneath her white satin comforter. That morning, she called Henry Weinstein, telling him she was too ill to make it to work that Monday. By 4 p.m. she sounded even worse, when Weinstein checked in again. By Sunday evening, he had to contact Cukor and explain that Monday's shoot would have to begin without Monroe.

The first actual day of production was April 23, 1962, but the cast and crew had to work around the star, after being informed that the

leading lady had come down with a severe sinus infection and could not make it to work that morning. The studio sent the staff doctor to confirm the illness on Sunday. Dr. Lee Siegel examined Monroe at her home and agreed with the diagnosis. His diagnosis and treatment called for rest, meaning the star couldn't step before the cameras. It was suggested that they postpone the filming of *Something's Got to Give* for a month, but Cukor didn't want to wait. The director opted to reorganize his shooting schedule, focusing on scenes that didn't require Monroe.

On April 23, at 7:30 a.m., Cyd Charisse was summoned to the Fox lot to film alongside Dean Martin in what would become the first scenes of *Something's Got to Give*. Cukor filmed Martin and Charisse talking to children as they build a tree house.

Over the next three weeks, filming of *Something's Got to Give* continued mostly without Monroe. The star did appear briefly on April 30 to film her entrance to the house. However, due to fever and head-aches from the sinusitis, as well as a bout with bronchitis, she was of little use. She appeared again on May 1, but reportedly fainted under the hairdryer and had to be taken home.

On May 7, she forced her driver to take her to the studio and arrived at 7:30 a.m. After a "shot" to boost her energy, she began to feel better and climbed into her makeup chair for hair and makeup, and then a Jean Louis print dress for her first scene.

At about 10:30 a.m., Monroe walked onto Soundstage 14 to film her first acting scene. She met the child actors she would be performing with and felt strong enough to work. "I remember looking up at her, and it was as if she drifted out of a mist," recalled Alexandria Heilweil, who portrayed her daughter in the film. "To this day she is the model of femininity to me."

Christopher Morely, who played her son, recalled her as a "glamorous mirage of strong perfume and the loveliest face I had seen before or since."

At 11 a.m., cameras finally rolled on Monroe. Monroe would

encounter her children for the first time since her character had been rescued from a tropical island, after having been lost at sea. It was to be a teary reunion for Monroe's character as she saw her young children having grown during her five-year absence, as they played around the pool, and not knowing she was their mother.

After a break for lunch, the crew reassembled to film a scene of Monroe reuniting with the family dog, Tippy. A nine-year-old cocker spaniel named Jeff was trained to bark on cue, at a signal from his owner. However, the scene was filmed over and over again, with the dog repeatedly missing its cue. The dog was supposed to bark twice and kiss her on the chin, but no matter how many times they filmed the scene, the dog missed its mark. Footage of the scene showed Monroe remaining composed and patient, and even playful during the filming. Monroe's love of animals was evident, and she clearly enjoyed working with the dog.

Marilyn was prepared for every line, but the dog failed to deliver. The cast and crew took an afternoon break, but tried again at 3:30 and spent another two hours trying to get the dog to perform. Some felt Cukor wasted valuable time on a scene that could have easily been completed with proper editing.

Cukor, reports say, was terribly unhappy with the current situation. Fox had forced him to fulfill the terms of his contract by making the film and when he tried to get out of it, they threatened legal action. Tying him up in court could have prevented Cukor from working and that was the last thing he wanted. Cukor was poised to begin work on what would become one of his proudest achievements. Rather than focusing on *Something's Got To Give*, some suggest he was already at work on his next picture, planning in his head, the feature film version of the hit Broadway play *My Fair Lady*.

My Fair Lady would be his 1964 Warner Bros. musical starring Audrey Hepburn. The challenge and opportunity the feature presented was both daunting and exciting. Cukor would ultimately go on to win the Academy Award for Best Director for the film, which would also become

1964's Best Picture of the Year. However, before he could head over to Warner Bros., he had to get through to Marilyn Monroe and complete *Something's Got To Give.*

Unfortunately for Cukor, on May 8, exhaustion got the better of Monroe, and she suffered a relapse. Doctors again ordered her to remain home – this time until May 14 – in order to fully recuperate. Cukor would have to shoot around her again. Soon, the production was behind

schedule by 10 days, and Fox saw it costing them money – money the studio didn't have.

With the production over budget and behind schedule, and the script still undergoing nightly rewrites, the director, cast and crew were growing frustrated. So was the front office.

Goddess & the Girl Next Door

eleven

"I've never fooled anyone. I've let people fool themselves. They didn't bother to find out who and what I was. Instead, they would invent a character for me. I wouldn't argue with them. They were obviously loving somebody I wasn't."

- Marilyn Monroe

"How naive I was when I made my first picture ... I played a girl who took a trip to South America. I kept expecting the cast to take off for the high seas, but the whole thing was shot on Stage 4 at the studio!"

- Doris Day

Something Gives.

The Studio, The Star & the Director Reach Their Breaking Points

After roughly one month of production, only about seven-and-a-half minutes of Monroe had been captured for *Something's Got to Give*. Some brief moments with her children, along with a scene where she is impersonating a Swedish housekeeper as Cyd Charisse and Dean Martin arrive home from their honeymoon, but not much else. On the rare occasions Marilyn appeared on the set that first month, she usually would be late and nervous about how she was going to be treated for not being there earlier or as often. When she appeared, she also wasn't interested in Cukor's direction, looking to her acting coach, Paula Strasberg, for affirmation, which only made things more intense.

Cukor quickly grew frustrated by Strasberg. When not on the set, Monroe spent most of her time locked in her dressing room with Strasberg. Cukor found Strasberg, "pretentious, ridiculous, and not very nice," and felt he would have a far better chance getting a performance out of Monroe had she not been around. Strasberg reportedly stood off camera for all of Monroe's scenes, and even when Cukor called "Cut," Monroe would wait for Strasberg to give her a signal that the scene was over.

Cukor felt method acting was a farce and resented Strasberg's interference. Strasberg knew she wasn't welcome on the set and it was made perfectly clear by the director that she was in the way. Her motiva-

tions, however, were not to defer to Cukor or to Fox. She was there only to provide Marilyn the emotional support and to represent her husband.

Cukor largely blamed Strasberg for upsetting Monroe's performance and making her character into something the film didn't really call for. According to Walter Bernstein, who was on the set for much of Monroe's filming, Monroe would confer with Strasberg before every scene in what he called "very serious" conversations, "and then Miss Monroe would carry this seriousness back into the scene where, since the picture was a comedy, it did not always fit."

Paula Strasberg was equally frustrated. According to her daughter Susan, when Paula accompanied Marilyn back to New York for the Kennedy gala, her mood was sour. "When mother arrived, she seemed to be suffering from life – If she ate, she got fat; if she helped, she was ridiculed; if she loved, she was rejected; if she dreamed, she was disillusioned."

By May, the film was closing in on a million dollars over-budget, and Monroe had been absent far more than she was present. During the star's absences, Cukor made the most of the situation by filming as many of the scenes of Dean Martin and Cyd Charisse that didn't require Monroe. When he ran out of material, he tried to film Martin's side of conversations his character would have with Monroe. For Martin's benefit, Cukor would use the script girl or anyone on set who was available, so Martin has someone whom to react to.

When Monroe did appear, late and wresting with guilt, she was apologetic about her tardiness. Some reports suggest that she was intensely afraid of facing the camera and was seen even throwing up before reaching the set. Producer Henry Weinstein, a witness to Monroe's episodes of fear, said, "We all experience anxiety, unhappiness, heartbreaks, but that was sheer, primal terror."

George Cukor knew that reprimanding Monroe would only make matters worse; so he simply tried to reassure her by telling her, "not to worry or be nervous, because she was worth waiting for."

When Monroe returned to the set on May 14, at 7:30 a.m., the studio wasn't expecting her. She had been absent the previous week, and Cukor was sure she wouldn't show. He was shocked when he received a call that she was on set, in makeup and ready to work. While Monroe had been absent much of the previous month, all her absences had been "excused" by the studio, because doctors advised her to stay home and rest. Fox's own studio physician confirmed she was, in fact, too ill to work.

Cukor would put her to work that day, but some on the set saw him intent on punishing the star. He reportedly spent every night re-working the script and sending over pages and pages of changes to her, expecting her to be prepared for the next day's shooting. The script had been altered so much that only four pages actually remained from the

original approved script before production began. Traditionally, a complete script of white pages is updated with changes printed on blue pages. Changes to the blue pages are then updated with pink pages.

To try and trip Monroe up, Cukor sent over changes on plain white paper, rather than the traditional blue paper that indicated changes. Monroe, however, caught on and remained prepared, going so far as to making her own changes to the new white pages in the script.

She wanted very much to finish the picture and be done with her

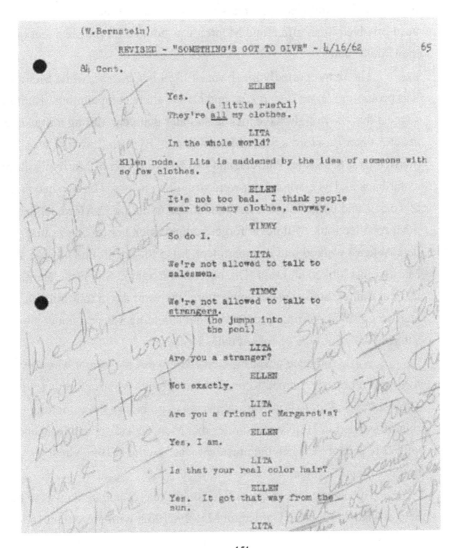

old Fox contact, but irritated at Cukor as much as Fox. Animosity on the set between Cukor, Monroe, Weinstein and Strasberg became one where cast and crew were asked to take sides, any many like Dean Martin and Cyd Charisse, tried to stay out of it. However, one event got in the way and would become an impasse that would lead to her firing.

The breaking point in production came when Monroe opted to fly to New York for President John F. Kennedy's Madison Square Garden birthday celebration. Few official details exist of the relationship between Marilyn and Kennedy; but stories suggest that the two might have been involved in an affair, and Monroe was hooked on the president of the United States.

The two reportedly met back as 1959 in Chicago, while Monroe was promoting *Some Like It Hot*, and he was there campaigning. Rumors suggest that they might have met again, later that year, during a weekend at actor Peter Lawford's Santa Monica home. By then, Lawford was married to JFK's sister, Patricia, and had been a friend of Marilyn's, from as far back as 1947, when both were struggling actors. The two had met at a party, and while Monroe never admitted to dating Lawford, he had other recollections. "I'll never forget going to pick her up on our first date. When I walked into the apartment, I had to step around the dog shit. Marilyn just looked and said 'Oh, he's done it again.' She just clammed up over dinner, but I saw her some more. We went down to Malibu in the jeep, to go surf-boarding. I remember her shielding her skin under a big sun hat. We went on a couple of dates I guess."

While romance never blossomed between the two, it was Lawford who reportedly helped Kennedy connect with Monroe. In fact, just as *Something's Got to Give* was preparing to go before the cameras, rumors swirled in Hollywood circles that Monroe had spent a weekend with JFK in March, when the president was staying at Bing Crosby's house in Palm Springs.

To celebrate the president's 45th birthday, a huge gala was to be held at Madison Square Garden on May 19, 1962, with more than 15,000 people in attendance. Both a fundraising opportunity and a chance to promote the democratic party and the president's impending reelection campaign, the event would including many Hollywood celebrities as well as powerful politicians. Marilyn was invited to appear.

With her new film requiring much of her focus, Monroe accepted the invitation to the event, but sought clearance to travel from Fox executives. Fox records show that studio executives approved Monroe's appearance at the event on April 9.

However, by mid-May, as Kennedy's birthday approached, *Something's Got to Give* was falling seriously behind schedule and over budget, and Monroe's absences from filming had been the main cause. Some felt it would be a mistake for her to leave the production to attend the event, knowing it would cause only further delays.

Monroe had been planning her special appearance for weeks. Scheduled to appear onstage at the end of the event to sing "Happy Birthday, Mr. President," and usher in a large birthday cake, Monroe personally designed a dress with help from designer Jean Louis. The dress was intended to make her the most talked about star of the evening. It was made of a sheer and flesh-colored marquisette fabric, with 2,500 crystals

and 6,000 shimmering rhinestones sewn onto it. It was so tightly fitted to her that Monroe was unable to wear anything underneath it. Monroe had spent $1,400 of her own money on the dress and more for a matching white stole. She had to be sewn into the top half before she could even go on stage. She had no intention of missing the event.

Fox studio counsel warned Monroe that leaving the production

and missing another day of shooting would bring her trouble. "If she had been well and appeared regularly on the set for the last three weeks, we would have said, 'God bless you, go ahead,'" said Peter Levathes. "As it was, she had been absent for most of three weeks and had just returned to work."

Monroe received a written two-page warning that threatened dismissal if she were to leave the production for New York. The letter even stated that it had been known on the set that Monroe planned to leave for the east coast at noon on Thursday. Those on the set, however, were not expecting Monroe to leave town. In fact, on May 13, gossip columnist Hedda Hopper called Fox's publicity chief Harry Brand to ask the studio about rumors she'd heard that Monroe would be attending the president's party in New York. Brand promised Hopper that he would check with the director and get back to her. Cukor assured him that Marilyn's attendance had been canceled, adding, "Dean Martin bowed out as well. We're too far behind."

Cukor had actually planned to film an elaborate dream sequence that Friday that featured a tropical island set, and the scene required both Monroe and Martin on set, along with Tom Tryon, her fellow tropical island castaway. The set had to be completed at least a day in advance because of water features, and actor Tom Tryon was schedule to work, after having been fitted with a sexy leopard-skin loincloth. "To say I was excited would be an understatement," recalled Tryon. "I was just getting started, and suddenly I had a chance to work with Marilyn Monroe."

However, Monroe discarded the studio warning. Just after noon on Thursday, a helicopter landed outside the set, with Peter Lawford jumping out and running into Soundstage 14 to fetch Monroe. Moments later, Monroe and Lawford appeared, along with Paula Strasberg and Pat Newcomb. The four boarded the helicopter for a short trip to LAX for the flight to New York. She had been on set a total of three and a half days, after having been ill for three weeks. Now she was gone. The elaborate fantasy sequence had to be canceled and the director, as well as the front office, was livid.

"Where the hell did she go?" asked Cukor to assistant director Buck Hall. "To sing 'Happy Birthday' to the president," he replied.

"But we settled all that! I said 'No,' the studio said 'No.' Period. She can't go."

But go she did. After two days of rehearsals, Marilyn Monroe would appear onstage at Madison Square Garden to sing to President Kennedy.

Peter Lawford was there to introduce Monroe, and made jokes about Marilyn's reputation for being late. When she at last appeared

at the end of the evening, Lawford introduced her as "the late Marilyn Monroe."

Marilyn walked out on stage, dropped a white ermine fur coat, and revealed the glittering skin-tight dress, to the president and attendees. The audience gasped. When President Kennedy got to the stage to thank the attendees, he remarked, "I can now retire from politics after having had Happy Birthday sung to me in such a sweet, wholesome way."

The event was a huge success for the star, but it was not well received back at Twentieth Century Fox. The wheels were in motion to fire her from *Something's Got to Give*. She just didn't know it yet.

Monroe and Paula Strasberg on the set.

twelve

"I sit in front of the mirror for hours looking for signs of age. Yet I like old people; they have great qualities that younger people don't have. I want to grow old without facelifts. They take the life out of a face, the character. I want to have the courage to be loyal to the face I've made. Sometimes I think it would be easier to avoid old age, to die young, but then you'd never complete your life, would you? You'd never wholly know yourself."

- Marilyn Monroe

"I can't bear to look at my rushes or my pictures, so I don't think I deserve it when nice things are said [about me]."

- Doris Day

Fired.

Monroe is Fired from 'Something's Got to Give'

On Sunday, May 20, Monroe flew back to Hollywood from New York; and by 6 a.m. Monday morning, she appeared at Soundstage 14,

161

prepared to work. She had messaged Cukor that she was prepared to film any one of the key seven scenes on the upcoming production schedule. However, she told him close-ups were out of the question. The hectic and busy weekend trip to New York had taken a toll on her face, and she feared it showed. Make-up might not be enough to hide how tired she really was.

While the news was good on the Monroe front, trouble came when Dean Martin reported to work complaining of a terrible cold and a temperature of 100 degrees. Since Cukor had scheduled a series of im-

portant dialogue scenes between Martin and Monroe, the schedule went to hell when Monroe refused to film with him. After consulting with the studio doctor and a specialist at Cedars of Lebanon, where Monroe had been treated for her sinus infection, they suggested she not be around Martin while he was ill.

Cukor complained that it was nonsense and Martin was not contagious; but Monroe locked herself in her dressing room and refused to appear if Martin were there. Eventually, Cukor brought Cyd Charisse in to work instead; and he only used Monroe for one small scene with her onscreen son, played by Christopher Morley.

On May 22, Martin remained ill, and Monroe told the studio by memo, "I cannot work with Mr. Martin until he's well. I take this action on advice from my physicians."

Cukor opted to use Monroe for half a day in a scene with Cyd Charisse. However, without Martin he was in a tight spot; because the bulk of the scenes required both him and Monroe together or with other actors. While there were some scenes Monroe could film without him – like her rescue at sea, oddly enough, Cukor chose not to film them.

Before Monroe left for the day on Tuesday, Cukor and she had a private conference to discuss a key scene for Wednesday. After Monroe's departure, Cukor cleared the soundstage and had the crew prepare for Wednesday. They would be filming Monroe's nude swim scene.

Pat Newcomb had prepared for the press-worthy event, calling photographer Lawrence Schiller the night before, telling him, "I would plan to be on the set all day tomorrow if I were you, Larry – and bring plenty of film. Marilyn has that swimming scene tomorrow and, knowing Marilyn, she might slip out of that suit."

In the *Something's Got to Give* script, Marilyn tries to tempt her husband by skinny-dipping in the pool late one evening. Cukor asked Marilyn to film the scene in a specially created flesh-colored bikini to give the appearance she was naked; but for additional publicity, Cukor convinced Monroe to lose the bikini and actually film the swim in the buff. Since Monroe had spent months getting into shape, trimming down and losing more than 20 pounds, she immediately agreed, even knowing photographers from *Life* magazine were on hand to capture the event. She had lost additional weight due to a reported gallbladder surgery months earlier.

Additional security was added to Fox's Soundstage 14 for the famous scene, and Cukor added a second film camera to capture the scene from two different angles. The set was cleared of any unnecessary crew or extras not required for the scene. Even the electricians who were required for the key lighting were reportedly asked to look away.

The nude scene garnered a great deal of publicity in newspapers and magazines, and would have helped the film in release. In fact, it

would have been the first major star nude scene in a major motion picture, had the film been completed.

"I had been wearing the flesh-colored suit," Monroe told one reporter, "but it concealed too much, and it would have looked wrong on the screen. "My birthday is June 1, and I thought I'd celebrate a little early by acting in my birthday suit."

Monroe was perfectly comfortable in the nude and held no reservations being seen by men or women, as she knew she was a beautiful woman. In fact, she was more concerned about her swimming skills than the nudity. "All I can do is dog-paddle," she told Cukor. "That will be just fine, darling," he replied.

After filming of the scene was completed, Monroe was photographed in the bikini bottom, as well as without it. The sensational shots would knock Elizabeth Taylor's romance with Richard Burton off the front of the tabloids. Monroe assumed the studio would be pleased with the publicity.

Fox executives got a chance to view the footage of the nude swim scene on Friday, May 25. The studio brass agreed it was sensational. Along with her skirt blowing up on the New York streets from *The Seven Year Itch*, this would be the scene that moviegoers would remember.

Monroe, doing her part as an eager employee, appeared on set every day that week. However, Cukor was still unable to get Martin and Monroe on camera together. Martin was still recovering from his cold, and Monroe refused to appear with him. Cukor suspected it had more to do with Monroe being tired from her busy schedule and wanted to look her best before any close-ups.

Between May 25 and June 1, Marilyn filmed 10 key scenes and worked nine days. However, on Friday afternoon, June 1, things began to unravel. A small birthday party was planned for Marilyn 36th birthday. During a break that afternoon, Monroe's publicist, Pat Newcomb, appeared on the set with a crystal glass of champagne for the star. Cukor demanded Newcomb "leave the set with that champagne" and that she should "act like a publicist and not a social director."

The cast and crew wanted to celebrate the event with a small surprise party, but Cukor refused, saying they needed to get in a full day's work. Monroe's stand-in Evelyn Moriarty went behind his back, buying a seven-dollar sheet cake at the Los Angeles Farmers Market. A studio illustrator drew a cartoon of a nude Monroe holding a towel, which read "Happy Birthday (Suit)" for an oversized birthday card, signed by the cast and crew. When they surprised the star on the set, Monroe was touched, but Cukor was not amused.

Cukor had worked Monroe fully that Friday. Along with Wally Cox and Dean Martin, the three filmed a lengthy sequence in which Monroe tries to pass Cox off as her desert island co-castaway. The scene was filmed 14 times. After Monroe's death, Cukor would claim that all the takes were useless. He said Monroe acted as if she were, "underwater," and that there was an "insane, hypnotic quality" to all the footage.

However, those that have viewed the scenes claim that Cukor had lied and that 13 of the scenes were nearly identical. The one that was a failure was not due to Monroe, but because Cox flubbed his line.

In fact, even though Cukor would claim that drugs and mental instability were the reason the star couldn't perform, those on the set claimed that it was script changes by Cukor that sabotaged the picture. It appeared that in scenes where Monroe had memorized the script she completed takes with little trouble; but for scenes where Cukor had submitted changes the evening before or sometimes that morning, Monroe had difficulty remembering her lines. There were some who suspected Cukor forced the take after take routine to push the budget overruns and to punish both Monroe and the studio. Others argued that Monroe had pushed him to the edge with her own behavior on the set and her ill feelings toward Fox.

Trying to put the animosity aside, the cast attempted to celebrate the star's birthday. However, even with the small impromptu celebration, Monroe sensed the hostility from Cukor. The cast decided to move the

party to Dean Martin's dressing room and left Cukor behind. Wally Cox asked Marilyn, "Do you feel thirty-six?"

Monroe replied, "I feel thirty-six and then some. And each day on this movie makes me feel older and older."

After the party, Monroe borrowed one of the Jean Louis outfits made for her for the film to wear for an appearance at Dodger Stadium that evening. Asking Henry Weinstein if she could wear the outfit, she said, "The suit is the only thing I've got that's warm enough."

A cold front had moved into southern California and temperatures dipped that evening. "You're not going through with that?" asked Weinstein. "The night air will kill you."

Even the studio doctor warned Monroe not to go out the stadium that evening, fearing she would have a relapse. "I have to go," Monroe told them. "The people from the Muscular Dystrophy Association have sold thousands of tickets. Besides, I promised to take Dean Martin's son."

As promised, Monroe made the benefit event, but suffered through the evening, even though she tried to appear upbeat. Los Angeles Angels center fielder, Albie Pearson, was selected to escort Monroe onto the field. Pearson recalled not knowing it was Monroe, at first. "There was some sort of charity function at the stadium, and I'm selected to escort a celebrity to home plate for a pregame presentation," Pearson said. "So I go out to the dugout, and they tell me the person I'm going to walk to home plate is Marilyn Monroe."

Pearson said that once he knew it was Marilyn Monroe, he suddenly got nervous, expecting some larger-than-life celebrity surrounded by press and people to show up. "So I ask, 'Where is she?' And it turned out, she was standing over in the far corner of the dugout, completely in the shadows. And she's pale and shaking and I'm thinking this can't be Marilyn Monroe, the famous movie star."

The ball player didn't think Monroe would actually make it through the evening, he said. "We're called out to home plate, and I thought I would have to drag her out of that corner. But once she hit that top step of the dugout, she became Marilyn Monroe the movie star, smiling and waving. I was simply amazed at the transformation."

He said Monroe never spoke to him during the publicity event. "Once we're back in the dugout, she turns back into this shy, withdrawn person," he recalled. "She looked so lost and lonely, and I felt I needed to say something; but what do you say to Marilyn Monroe?"

By the end of the evening, the chill had gotten to her, and her sinus infection had returned. That Monday, when Monroe failed to show up for work, the studio began the process of firing her. Fox had invested roughly $2.1 million in *Something's Got to Give*, and Monroe had not lived up to the terms of her contract by leaving production for the Kennedy gala. Now, by failing to show up for work, she had pushed the studio to its breaking point. While her previous absences had been excused, this one was not. Soon, the Fox lawyers and executives on both coasts were on conference calls to decide what to do. George Cukor was brought in for his assessment of the situation. Cukor told the executives that he didn't think he had enough useful output from Monroe to "fashion into a coherent film."

Cukor said he resented "Marilyn's shenanigans, her plotting, bullying and outsmarting the studio, making outrageous demands, and the studio stupidly giving in on every point."

Whether Cukor believed it or was just using his words to punish Monroe and Fox, the damage was done. His assessment sealed Monroe's fate and on Friday, June 8, court documents were filed that Marilyn Monroe was in breach of her contract with Fox and was fired from *Something's Got to Give*.

Dean Martin got word of Monroe's firing while on set. At about 3:45 p.m., hairstylist Ages Flanaghan entered Dean's dressing room to ask him if he'd heard that Kim Novak was replacing Monroe as his new costar. "I don't think so, honey. I'd certainly have heard about that."

A short time later the studio call sheet was posted, saying "Set closed until further notice – Per instructions from the legal department."

Next, Marilyn's make-up artist, Whitey Snyder confronted Dean, who was still wearing his golf clothes after playing a round at the Los Angeles Country Club. "Dean, I think they've fired Marilyn," said Snyder.

Snyder told Dean he'd learned from the front office that Lee Remick was already being fitted for costumes to replace Monroe. Martin asked his assistant to head over to the production office to, "Find out what the hell was going on." She returned a few minutes later, saying, "Yep. Monroe's been fired, and Lee Remick is going to be your new leading lady."

Lee Remick actually owed Fox two films, so the studio had her on contract as a replacement for Monroe, with the hope that Dean Martin could sell the comedy all by himself. Martin, however, had other plans. "I made a contract to do this picture with Marilyn Monroe. That's the deal, the only deal," he told Snyder. "We're not going to be doing it with Lee Remick or any other actress."

Dean Martin's contract guaranteed that he would star opposite Monroe. She had been instrumental in getting him the part, over Fox's desire to cast James Garner. Martin would side with Marilyn over the studio and Cukor. Martin walked off the set as soon as he'd found out, and by the time he arrived at home, United Press International was there asking for a comment. "I have the greatest respect for Miss Remick as an artist, but I signed to do this film with Marilyn Monroe."

Things were looking bleaker by the minute at Fox.

thirteen

"I've never fooled anyone. I've let people fool themselves. They didn't bother to find out who and what I was. Instead they would invent a character for me. I wouldn't argue with them. They were obviously loving somebody I wasn't."

- Marilyn Monroe

-

"Work with me is therapy, a way to release this energy."

- Doris Day

Rehired.

Fox Re-Thinks Its Situation in Monroe's Favor

Fox had initially hoped a holiday release over Christmas would provide a much-needed source of revenue from *Something's Got to*

Give for the studio coffers. With the cost of *Cleopatra* exceeding every imaginable figure and no end in sight for when the picture would be completed, let alone arrive in movie theaters, the studio felt its hands were tied. The decision to fire Monroe, according to many key players at Fox at the time, was influenced by the fact that it had lost control of *Cleopatra*. Off on location and embroiled in a battle of wills and publicity over the costly picture, Fox could only show strength by punishing Monroe. Showing its serious side might enable them to get *Cleopatra* back on track, and at this point, Monroe has provided little to *Something's Got to Give*. It was reported that Cukor had only captured about seven minutes of usable footage of Monroe in the film. So, with that, they felt their best recourse was to fire her.

Though Monroe's firing was officially recorded on June 7, word had leaked out by June 6 with gossip and rumors that the star was being dropped from the film. Scriptwriter Nunnally Johnson already had cabled studio chief Peter Levathes, suggesting Cukor might be the better one to fire, rather than Monroe. "If you're going to take anybody out of this picture, shouldn't you decide first who brings people in, George Cukor or Marilyn Monroe? You should remove George, because they are so antipathetic and that's what's causing Marilyn's disturbance."

Marilyn, learning of her fate, immediately flew into action, knowing the Fox publicity machine would go to work against her. She retaliated by giving interviews to newspapers and magazines with her side of the story. As expected, Fox countered her through the press, suggesting Monroe was unstable, unprofessional and incapable of completing their film or fulfilling the terms of her contract.

On June 7, Marilyn's face appeared on the front page of the *New York Post*, with the headline, "Marilyn Monroe Fired-Says She's Ill."

About the same time, reports that Fox was preparing a replacement forced Marilyn to make it clear that she was prepared to complete the film. The studio was notified by her attorney that Monroe was "ready and eager to go back to work on Monday, June 11."

The studio issued a formal announcement on Monroe's dismissal, saying it was necessary because of her, "repeated, willful breaches of her contract." The studio claimed that Monroe provided no justification for repeated failures to report for work, causing the studio to suffer serious financial losses. Fox filed a $750,000 lawsuit against her.

Fox already had been working secretly to find a suitable replacement. On Monday, June 4 the studio contacted Kim Novak over at Columbia, to see if they might convince her to come on board. Novak, who herself had been treated poorly by front office executives and powerful studio men, refused to fill Monroe's shoes.

On Tuesday, they reached out to Shirley MacLaine, who also refused to take the part. On Wednesday, they contacted Doris Day. Doris was reluctant to take the role for several reasons. Not only did she not like the idea of trying to replace Marilyn Monroe, but also she had concerns that the script might not be right for her. It wasn't a difficult decision and in just a few hours, she responded to them, declining the part.

By Thursday, Lee Remick became the odd one out. Fox offered her $80,000 to star in the picture, but Remick suspected this might be more about publicity than the film. She agreed to do the movie, provided they pay her the full amount after signing the contract. If Monroe stepped back into the role, she wanted to be paid in full. Remick was already scheduled to film *The Running Man* in July, but she had a feeling she'd never set foot on a Fox soundstage to film *Something's Got to Give*; so she didn't cancel the assignment. It was a wise move on her part.

When Fox suggested Lee Remick as a replacement, Dean Martin said that, although he had the greatest respect for her talents, he "signed to do the picture with Miss Monroe," Martin said, "and will do it with no one else."

Fox had no choice but to close down production until they figured out what to do.

Marilyn sent a telegram to Cukor on June 8 that said: "Dear George, Please forgive me, it was not my doing. I had so looked forward to working with you." Monroe sent nearly identical telegrams to co-stars Dean Martin and Cyd Charisse, and another to the larger cast and crew.

By June 11, with no plans to resume the film, Cukor and associate producer Gene Allen packed their belongings at Fox and walked off the lot. Although Cukor's 26-week contract had ended, he was placed on a week-to-week salary.

"The picture is in a state of contingency; there was no salary and we cannot accept other jobs," Cukor told a reporter, "We just sit and wait." He was relieved by the turn of affairs, because, as he said, "even if we'd finished the picture, it would not have been much good."

Cukor told columnist Hedda Hopper that no company would accept Monroe's antics. He suggested that she was "over the hill," and it might have contributed to her erratic behavior. He said that he felt enormously sorry for her, but he saw her as, "a dangerous girl." Cukor told Hopper, "Marilyn has these stooges around who dislike her really. The terrifying thing was that she wanted to do the picture, but she had no control of herself."

Cukor was upset that the picture was canceled after Dean Martin refused to accept anyone but Monroe. Cukor perceived him as a, "dis-

ciple of Sinatra."

"Martin declared that Monroe was in his contract and refused to proceed with Remick. Before production stopped, Martin bellyached to Cukor about how impossible it was to work with Marilyn," wrote Hopper.

"Fox was weak and stupid and deserved everything it got," Cukor reportedly told Hopper. "But Marilyn deserved what she got, too." Cukor told the columnist that Marilyn couldn't remember her lines, acting as though she were under water, and in the afternoon, she was under the influence of alcohol."

On its June 22 cover, *Life* magazine featured Marilyn, wrapped in a blue terrycloth robe, with the headline, "The skinny dip you'll never see."

However, behind the scenes, there was work on getting her nude scene onto movie screens by reinstating Monroe and completing the film. Having invested millions and garnered a massive amount of publicity over the star and the picture, Fox thought there was a good chance they could bring Monroe back, ensuring she would be on her best behavior and committed to completing the film, which was further along in production than some suggested.

Executives had seen all footage from the shoot, including the last day's work with Monroe, Martin and Cox, and agreed Monroe's performance was stronger than Cukor admitted. They suspected they might be able to use the firing as a scare tactic to get Monroe to shape up. Nunnally Johnson may have been right all along – and Cukor was the one who had to go.

In fact, on Wednesday, July 25, 1962, screenwriter Hal Kanter submitted a revised version of the script for *Something's Got To Give* to Peter Levathes. Levathes, Fox's head of production, intended on presenting Marilyn the revised script at her home. Levathes hoped he could use the new script as a way to build a bridge to Monroe to restart the production and Fox would agree to rehire her. Levathes told Monroe he wanted a clean slate so they could start over. Fox had decided to rehire Marilyn Monroe.

Levathes recalled the meeting, years later, as the last time he saw the star. "As so often with Marilyn's history at Fox, we simply decided to reinstate her. I was the one responsible for firing her; so, I wanted to be the one to personally rehire her. No one wanted bad blood. She told me she didn't want her name tarnished, nor did she wish to ruin anyone."

Wanting to look her best that evening, Marilyn had her makeup done by friend and makeup artist Whitey Snyder. Hollywood hair stylist Agnes Flanagan, who had been working with Monroe on *Something's Got To Give,* washed and styled her hair. Since Levathes was coming to her home for the meeting, Marilyn wanted someone there to listen to conversation, but not to intrude on the private meeting. She asked her publicist, Pat Newcomb, to eavesdrop on the meeting behind a bedroom door.

When Levathes arrived at her home, Marilyn was focused on a vast array of photos of her by Bert Stern and George Barris. Contact sheets and larger prints were placed in rows covering much of the floor. She walked in and out of the rows, studying the images and making

decisions about which ones to use for press and media requests. Marilyn welcomed Levathes in and invited his opinion in helping her select the best shots.

Levathes told Marilyn that the lawsuits would be dropped and she would be reinstated at a higher salary, and she was relieved to hear the news. However, Fox insisted that Marilyn's team, including Paula Strasberg, Dr. Greenson and Pat Newcomb, would be kept off the set if production was to resume. She agreed.

He recalled his last meeting with Marilyn as a positive one. "She did not seem unhappy or depressed at all, she asked if we could review the new script and we did. She read it and was very astute about it, thinking carefully before she made some excellent suggestions."

Marilyn suggested adding a comedic scene that showed how her character's time away from civilization left an impact on her. "A woman who has been off on a desert island for years wouldn't eat so delicately with knives and forks," so Marilyn felt it might be more humorous to show her eating with her hands. "And she suggested another scene in which her character just forgot about shoes, because she was unused to wearing them," recalled Levathes. "I remember saying, 'Marilyn, these are beautiful ideas!' She was very happy and creative and glad to have a say in the revised script. She was in fine spirits and looking forward to getting back to work."

As the meeting came to a close, Levathes said goodbye as Marilyn returned to the task of once again selecting photographs of herself. "This was not, I thought, a shallow person, and I was sorry I never really knew her," Levathes would say. "She was a woman who made distinctions, who thought about her life, who knew the difference between sham and reality. She had depth. Of course, she was enormously complex, and I had a sense of some real underlying suffering there."

Levathes would never see Marilyn again and would recall the poignancy of their final time together. "[A]t her best, there was no one like her. The wounds with Fox were healed, and when I last saw her, she was like a young and beautiful starlet, eager to do a picture that now had real possibilities."

An interview with *Life* magazine by Richard Meryman was published on August 3, 1962 — just two days before Monroe's death, had the star reflecting on recent events. "Fame is fickle," she told the writer. "I now live in my work and in a few relationships with the few people I can really count on. Fame will go by, and so long, I've had you, fame. If it goes by, I've always known it was fickle. So, at least it's something I experienced, but that's not where I live."

With no other pictures on the schedule, Fox knew it would take a little time to get *Something's Got to Give* back off the ground. So, the studio wanted to rush Darryl Zanuck's big-budget war epic, *The Longest Day,* into an early release. Zanuck's intense account of the Allied invasion of Normandy on June 6, 1944, had a large international cast of stars, including Richard Burton, Henry Fonda, Eddie Albert, Red Buttons, Sean Connery, Mel Ferrer, Jeffrey Hunter, Peter Lawford, John Wayne and more. If Fox could get it into theaters, it might give the studio some much needed cash – cash it needed for completing both *Cleopatra* and *Something's Got to Give.*

Zanuck, Fox's largest shareholder, had labored over *The Longest Day* for years and wasn't thrilled with the idea of pushing the picture out before it was ready, and he balked at the idea. Fearing Fox would push *The Longest Day* out before he was finished with it, Zanuck used his power to regain control of Fox, replacing Spyros Skouras as president. Skouras was accused of failing to stop the massive cost overruns of *Cleopatra* that were responsible for the studio's precarious state – the brink of bankruptcy. He was blamed also for the debacle that forced the studio to shelve *Something's Got To Give.* Zanuck promptly made his son, Richard D. Zanuck, head of production, and the men got to work rebuilding the once powerhouse studio.

Since *Something's Got to Give* could not be completed without Monroe and Martin, Fox executives decided that their best chance at survival was to re-sign Monroe and to finish *Something's Got to Give.* Marilyn would reportedly earn an additional $150,000 if she completed the film, putting her at a salary of $250,000, and $500,000 for a subsequent picture. Monroe was back.

While Marilyn was focused on her troubles at Fox, Doris wanted no part of *Something's Got To Give.* She was busy over at Universal, trying to recreate the success of *Pillow Talk* with James Garner in *The Thrill of It All.* Producer Ross Hunter again lured Day into the film with a promise of light comedy that showcased her innate comedic abilities and lacked the emotional strain he put her through for *Midnight Lace*. *The Thrill of It All* would be a romantic comedy directed by Norman Jewison. It would be Jewison's second of a seven-picture deal for Universal. The screenplay was written by Larry Gelbart and Carl Reiner.

The idea for the film came after a chance meeting between Ross Hunter and Carl Reiner at a dinner party in the early 1960s. Reiner originally had conceived the idea as a film for Judy Holliday. Holiday had scored big with films like *Born Yesterday* and *Bells Are Ringing*, and she had actually accepted the role, but dropped out of the film after discovering that she had breast cancer. Holliday would die of cancer at the age of 43 in 1965.

Day could easily fill Holliday's shoes and Universal was eager to get her back before the cameras. Her husband, Marty Melcher, was only too happy to cash the checks for her services.

For *The Thrill of It All,* Doris plays Beverly Boyer, the wife of Dr. Gerald Boyer, played by James Garner. A leading New York obstetrician, he helps Mr. and Mrs. Fraleigh with their goal of becoming parents. Edward Andrews and Arlene Francis, as the Fraleighs, are wealthy owners of a company that produces soap products, who invite the Boyers to a dinner party to celebrate their impending child. Beverly inadvertently impresses the Fraleigh's elderly father, the soap magnate and he hires her to appear as herself in TV commercials to promote his Happy Soap. Comedy ensues as her success surpasses their wildest expectations, both financially and in fame. Soon, as Dr. Boyer finds he's being recognized as the husband of the "Happy Soap" star, marriage troubles arise.

Jewison recalled that Marty Melcher told him that Doris would be fine on the movie under one condition. "All you gotta do is keep telling her that she looks great," said Melcher. "Remember that. She looks great. You won't have any trouble."

The director would later find his advice was on point. "They were Doris' weak point. Not her looks per se, but the way she perceived them. Doris did not believe she was an attractive woman. I thought she was beautiful. Millions of fans thought she was beautiful. Everybody she had ever worked with thought she was beautiful. She remained unconvinced."

To keep Doris convinced, cinematographer Russell Metty became the crucial figure in making Doris look her best. Metty had worked with Day on both *Midnight Lace* and *That Touch of Mink*, as well as Marilyn Monroe on *The Misfits*. He had worked also for producer Ross Hunter several times before, making Lana Turner look her best in both *Imitation of Life* and *Portrait in Black*.

For *The Thrill of It All*, Metty used a combination of strong lighting and soft filters to wash out Day's complexion. In her close-ups, all the freckles, blemishes, and wrinkles were washed away. "She'd have the skin of a teenager," said Jewison.

Still, Jewison said when production began, Day was nervous. "She seemed uneasy in the first scenes we shot. She couldn't relax into the role, and I suspect it was her anxiety about her looks.

Some have suggested that, like Monroe, Doris was aware that she was fast approaching middle age, and playing a housewife with young children and pregnancy would only increase attention on how old she was. If she came off too aged to pull off the part, critics could be harsh, and her popularity with moviegoers could suffer. However, *The Thrill of It All* would be a huge hit, and soon Fox would be looking to recapture lightning in a bottle by recasting Day and Garner for another picture after tragedy struck.

fourteen

"Beneath the makeup and behind the smile I am just a girl who wishes for the world."

- Marilyn Monroe

"The really frightening thing about middle age is the knowledge that you'll grow out of it."

- Doris Day

Looking Ahead.

Monroe Looks Ahead As Her Film Career Gets Back on Track

With *That Touch of Mink* topping the box office charts in June 1962 and a December release set for her next film, *Billy Rose's Jumbo*, Doris was focusing on *The Thrill of It All* as her next starring role. In addition, she hadn't forgotten about her music career.

To appease fans of her voice, Day was about to release a new album, *You'll Never Walk Alone*, in September. In addition, she was preparing for a duets album with musical composer and arranger James Harbert. She would be traveling downtown to Columbia Records' recording studios on Sunset Boulevard to lay down her side of tracks for a studio recording of *Annie Get Your Gun*. While it had been years since the Broadway show had left the stage and well over a decade since the film version had lit up the screen, Irving Berlin's musical score was still popular and well suited to Day's vocals.

Columbia had been doing a series of albums based on popular musicals with artists it had under contract. To complement Day, she was paired with Robert Goulet for the duets. Goulet was in New York,

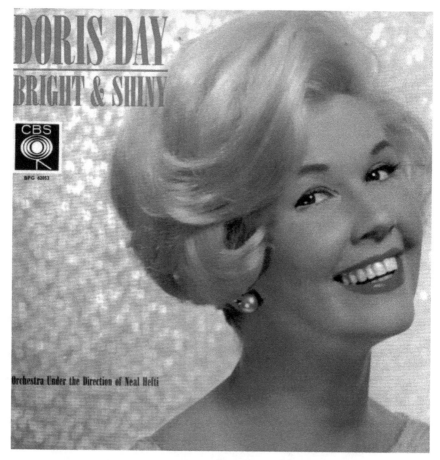

recording his portion of the tracks, and it was there that the album actually would be mixed. Day's Hollywood commitments prevented her from traveling to New York, so she opted to work out of downtown LA, with her tracks being shipped off to New York for merging with Goulet's vocals. She would complete the project in early October.

Meanwhile, with her film career looking to rebound, Marilyn accepted an invitation from Peter Lawford to head out of LA to spend a long weekend in Lake Tahoe at the Cal-Neva Lodge. Frank Sinatra was performing there, and Marilyn thought the getaway would do her good.

Built in 1926 by wealthy San Francisco businessman Robert P. Sherman, Cal-Neva became an important link between Nevada and the Hollywood entertainment industry. In 1935, 13-year-old Frances Gumm performed there with her sisters and caught the attention of songwriter Burton Lane. A few months later, Gumm signed a long-term contract with MGM and changed her name to Judy Garland. By the 1950s, under the ownership of Wingy Grober, the Cal-Neva would find Hollywood and powerful politicians mingling together as the Kennedy dynasty began to show up. Grober was a close friend of patriarch Joseph P. Kennedy. The extended Kennedy clan, including President John F. Kennedy and Attorney General Robert Kennedy would use Cal-Neva as a place to escape the high-pressure world of politics.

In 1960, Frank Sinatra became an owner of Cal-Neva and built the Celebrity Room Theater where he could perform. He installed a helicopter pad on the roof for his connected celebrities like Monroe and the Kennedys. Sinatra also performed with Dean Martin. Sammy Davis Jr., who would also use the resort as a vacation spot when not on stage. Judy Garland, Clara Bow, Will Rogers and the McGuire Sisters could be spotted there. While Doris Day didn't frequent the locale, Sinatra did look to her for advice when obtaining a loan for the investment. Day had secured a similar loan from the teamsters, so Frank "asked her if she had had to cut anybody in." She told him, "it was not necessary, it was a straight loan."

The last weekend in July, Marilyn called Joe DiMaggio and asked him to meet her at the Cal-Neva. She kept a low profile most of the weekend, but did attend Sinatra's show and spent time with Dean Martin, whom she thanked for his support during the troubles over *Something's Got to Give.* The two also discussed his co-starring with her in Fox's *I Love Louisa.* In addition, Martin and Monroe were expected to film *Kiss Me Stupid.* Director Billy Wilder hoped to bring Jack Lemmon and Monroe back together, after the smash, *Some Like It Hot.* Dean Martin would play the leading man with Lemmon in a supporting role. The role of Polly the Pistol had been written with Marilyn in mind.

While Marilyn spent much of her time in the privacy of one of the 219 guest rooms, she was spotted eating dinner and walking around the pool late one night with DiMaggio.

Sunday evening, July 29, Marilyn returned to Hollywood with the Lawfords, while DiMaggio went back to San Francisco. DiMaggio told friends that he and Marilyn had agreed to re-marry and set a date for August 8, 1962, in Los Angeles.

On Monday July 30, Marilyn reportedly agreed to make *I Love Louisa* with J. Lee Thompson as director, after completing *Something's Got to Give*. The production would start early 1963. If the script to *Goodbye Charlie* met with her approval, the film production would follow.

Also that Monday, Marilyn contacted her lawyer, Milton Rudin, about updating her will. She had signed her current will back on January 14, 1961, 10 days before her Mexican divorce from Arthur Miller was finalized. With her new contract coming from Fox, it would mean a significant hike in her financial status. Rumors were also out that she planned to change the current beneficiaries in her estate, including bequeaths to the Strasbergs.

Milton A. "Mickey" Rudin was a powerful entertainment lawyer whose name was associated with many celebrity clients and Hollywood powerhouses. In addition to Monroe, Rudin's clients included Frank Sinatra, Lucille Ball, Warner Bros., Desilu Studios and Elizabeth Taylor. Rudin did not want Marilyn to sign a new will because he was not sure she was thinking clearly at the time. He believed her addiction to drugs clouded her judgment and was the cause of what he saw as paranoia. The updated will was never filed.

On the last day of July, Marilyn had a final fitting for a dress designed for her by Jean Louis – rumored to be for her wedding – that morning and spent the afternoon with her psychoanalyst, Dr. Ralph Greenson. She typically appeared at Greenson's Santa Monica home at 4 p.m., driven over in a limo. Usually wearing dark glasses and her head covered by a scarf, she discreetly arrived for regular 90-minute session. After the session that day, she returned home and spent the next few hours on the phone.

Nunnally Johnson reportedly told director Jean Negulesco on August 1, that Negulesco was about to be asked to replace George Cukor on *Something's Got To Give*. Johnson said that Monroe had worked things out with Fox and she would be returning to the studio to complete the film, with the production due to kick off again at the end of October.

Marilyn's stand in, Evelyn Moriarty, phoned the star after hearing she was going back to work. Moriarty found Monroe "in great spirits" and recalled she was happy to be going back to work.

Rumors swirled through Monroe's small circle of her plans to remarry DiMaggio. She reportedly was planning a simple ceremony, with the dress from Jean Louis, followed by a catered reception and then honeymoon. She would return to complete *Something's Got to Give* in October.

Marilyn at home in her house at
Fifth Helena Drive in 1962.

fifteen

Goddess & the Girl Next Door

"The nicest thing for me is sleep, then at least I can dream."
- Marilyn Monroe

-

"I think whatever you need is within you, everything you need is there."
- Doris Day

The Last Day.

Mystery Surrounds the Death of Marilyn Monroe

The sky was bright blue and light shimmered off the swimming pool that morning as Eunice Murray arrived for work. It was August 4, 1962 and just after 8 a.m. when Murray stepped through the doorway

199

at Marilyn's home at Fifth Helena in Brentwood. Murray had spent the previous night in her Santa Monica apartment, but planned to stay over Saturday night, because there was much to do in the house, including deliveries and unpacking.

Marilyn was awake early that Saturday morning, after having slept poorly the night before. She looked tired. She appeared in the kitchen around 9 a.m., wearing her white terry cloth robe. She poured herself a glass of grapefruit juice. She told Murray that her houseguest, Pat Newcomb, was in the guest bedroom suffering from a cold. Neighbors would later note that they heard terrible coughing coming from Monroe's house that evening, which would later be attributed to Newcomb. Marilyn suggested the cold "could be baked out by a day beside the pool."

By 10 a.m., photographer Lawrence Schiller arrived at the home to talk about a request to use some photographs of Monroe for a

magazine article. Schiller was one of the three photographers present for Marilyn's naked swim on the set of *Something's Got To Give*. He found Marilyn intently working on her flowerbed in the front of her house as he pulled up in front. He recalled her as, "seemingly without a care that morning." She gave him a tour of her guest cottage as they discussed the photographs and project on Schiller's mind. She had recently completed remodeling and Marilyn was proud of the work she had put into the house and was in love with the vintage hacienda. To get the designs just right, she had even made a trip to Mexico in early 1962 so she could hand-select authentic art, tapestries and tiles for her new home. Some of the items purchased on the Mexico trip had just recently been delivered and were still wrapped in shipping materials, waiting to be unpacked.

Schiller and Monroe discussed the photos for the magazine, and Monroe marked her approved shots using a grease pencil. She spent the rest of the morning on the phone with friends, including Ralph Roberts, with whom she was planning a barbeque for Sunday evening. She was busy with arrangements and calls to a wine store and a caterer, and she had to sign for several deliveries.

Shortly before noon, Pat Newcomb, who had spent the night in one of her guest rooms, appeared and found Marilyn's mood had changed. "Marilyn seemed angry that I had been able to sleep and she hadn't – but something else was behind it all," recalled Newcomb. Some suspected that Newcomb's restful night was attributed to Monroe giving her Nembutal to help her rest. Monroe reportedly had a bottle of 25 pills recently prescribed by one of her many doctors and she would find the bottle with 24 pills remaining in the guest bedroom later that evening. The pill had put Newcomb in a deep sleep that lasted well into the morning – the kind of sleep Monroe longed for.

According to those close to her, Monroe spent the remainder of that last day on the phone. She had spoken at length with Marlon Brando and her former manager-producer, Milton Greene. Greene recalled the conversation, because she hadn't spoken to him in years. During the rare conversation, she confided in him that she was paranoid about the Strasbergs. She told him she "felt they had been using her," and said she was in the process of changing her will. There were also rumors that she planned on firing Paula Strasberg as her acting coach, dropping her analyst, Ralph Greenson, and firing her housekeeper, Eunice Murray. However, speculation has gone on for years about how much truth there was to some of this, as Monroe could be erratic and her intentions could change from one moment to the next. However, knowing her new arrangement with Fox, it was quite possible that Greenson and Strasberg

were out of the picture. If Greenson were gone, Eunice Murray couldn't be far behind, since he had been the one who brought her on board; and she and Marilyn had never really hit it off.

Newcomb joined Marilyn by the pool for lunch, and Eunice Murray recalled hearing them arguing. Newcomb confirmed the argument, saying that even though Marilyn claimed she was upset because Pat had slept well, Newcomb thought there might be more to it. "She was furious, it's true," Newcomb recalled. "But I think that she was also furious about something else, I think there was a lot more, not related to me, that I don't know about."

Much mystery surrounds the remainder of the day, with some speculating about a series of nefarious meetings and guests that never have fully been confirmed. Eunice Murray claimed at one time that Robert Kennedy visited Monroe, along with Peter Lawford, but in initial interviews, never mentioned their arrival. She later said they had arrived unannounced, early that last afternoon. However, many question her statements, because Kennedy was photographed with his family at a ranch outside San Francisco. Peter Lawford's neighbor, Ward Woods, also reported seeing Kennedy that day; yet Pat Newcomb said that to her knowledge, Kennedy did not visit Marilyn the last day of her life.

One visitor she did have that last day was Dr. Ralph Greenson, who arrived at the house about 1 p.m. that afternoon and had a private conversation with Monroe in her bedroom. Newcomb remained at Marilyn's, spending the afternoon sunbathing by the pool, while Monroe spoke with Greenson. Greenson left at about 3 p.m. for a brief trip home, but returned at 4:30 and stayed with Marilyn until 7 p.m.

According to Pat Newcomb, Greenson asked Eunice Murray to take Marilyn out for a walk on the beach. Murray drove Marilyn to Peter Lawford's beach house and left her there for about an hour while she went shopping for groceries.

Producer William Asher recalled seeing Marilyn at the Lawfords. "I was there along with a few other people who had dropped by. When

Marilyn arrived and took a walk on the beach."

Asher recalled that Marilyn appeared drugged when she arrived. She was "not staggering, but clearly under the influence, and she wasn't too steady in the sand."

Marilyn watched part of a volleyball game on the beach and left

after 4 p.m.; but an hour later, Peter Lawford called Marilyn and invited her back to the house for a casual dinner party with a few friends. Marilyn declined.

The Los Angeles Herald Examiner on Aug. 6, 1962, quoted Dr. Greenson as saying, "Marilyn had talked with me at 5:50 p.m., Saturday evening (Aug. 4, 1962.) She appeared distraught. I told her to take a drive and relax."

However, Greenson's story conflicts with Pat Newcomb's recollections. On Aug. 15, 1962, she told the *Herald Examiner* a different story. "Saturday she was getting things done inside the house-she loved it. This was the first home she ever owned herself. She was as excited about it as a little girl with a new toy when I last saw her at 6:30 p.m.," Newcomb recalled. "Nothing about her mood or manner had changed. She said to me, 'I'll see you tomorrow. Toodle-loo'."

However, after an afternoon therapy session, Greenson claimed that he left Marilyn's home at 7 p.m., and only Marilyn and her housekeeper were in the home.

Monroe reportedly had three final known calls that night. She had a pleasant conversation with Joe DiMaggio Junior, who had tried to reach her several times that day. They spoke for about 10 minutes, around 7:15 p.m., and he shared with her that he had broken off his engagement. Marilyn felt this was the right thing to do because she didn't think the girl was right for him. DiMaggio recalled Monroe as, "alert, happy and in good spirits."

Marilyn reportedly called Greenson right after speaking to DiMaggio. Greenson also recalled Marilyn was, "quite pleasant and more cheerful."

Her last known call came at about 7.40 p.m., and it was from Peter Lawford. Lawford was still trying to convince Marilyn to come to his house. The two spoke for about five minutes, and he claimed she sounded disoriented and her speech was slurred. He said he had to "shout to get her to pay attention" and asked her what was wrong. The call ended about 7.45 p.m., and he described a very different Marilyn than others who had spoken to her that evening. He said she was muttering, her speech was thickened, slurred and almost inaudible; she sounded distressed and disoriented. He claimed her last words to him were, "Say goodbye to Pat, say goodbye to the President, and say goodbye to yourself, because you're a nice guy."

The called ended at 7:45 p.m.

Peter Lawford claimed he called back but only got a busy signal. He said he then called back repeatedly for the next 30 minutes and eventually contacted the operator to try to interrupt the call. The operator reportedly told him the phone was either off the hook or out of order. Worried, but not wanting to get drawn into a scandal, because he was the brother-in-law of the president; Lawford said he called business manager Milton Ebbins, to see if he could go over to Marilyn's house and check on her. Ebbins called Marilyn's attorney Mickey Rudin, but no visit by either was reported.

Reports on what happened afterwards conflict with one another, and speculation goes from a murder conspiracy, to an intentional suicide, to an accidental overdose. Housekeeper Eunice Murray said that she first became alarmed when she noticed light coming from beneath Marilyn's door around midnight. She said the door was locked, and she got no response from Marilyn after repeated knocking. She phoned Dr. Greenson, who arrived about 12:30 a.m. Looking through Monroe's bedroom window, he saw her sprawled naked and unconscious on the bed. He said he broke the window and climbed inside where he found her lifeless and clutching the phone. He called her doctor who came shortly after and pronounced her dead. The police, however, were not called until 4:25 a.m.

Los Angeles Police Sergeant Jack Clemmons didn't normally answer calls to the police station, but he happened to be closest to the phone at 4:25 a.m. on August 5. When he picked up the phone, the caller told him Marilyn Monroe was dead. Clemmons received the call from

Greenson, who explained that he was Monroe's doctor and found her dead at her home in Brentwood of an apparent suicide.

It was also not his normal routine to rush to the scene of a suicide; but in this case he decided it was best to go himself. If it were Monroe, all hell would break loose with the press. If it weren't he didn't want to create a story of something that turned out to be a hoax. He arrived at the house minutes later and was invited in by Eunice Murray, who identified herself as the housekeeper. She took him to see the body.

Confirming it was Monroe's home and, in fact, her body, Clemmons verified the identities of those in the house at the time, which included Murray, Greenson and Dr. Hyman Engelberg, Marilyn's physician. Clemmons noted Monroe was lying naked and face down on her bed, arms at her sides. Her body was laying diagonally on the bed with her toes to the bottom right of the mattress and her head at the top left. A sheet had covered her, but he could see her face and her platinum hair, verifying it was indeed Marilyn Monroe.

Clemmons asked who found the body and Murray spoke up, saying she found her at about midnight. When he questioned as to why it took so long to contact the police, Greenson explained that the doctor was called, and that the publicity department at Fox was contacted first, because this would be a delicate situation for the studio. Clemmons was not pleased with the excuse, but it was what it was. Eight to ten empty bottles of prescription medication were on her bedside table and Greenson surmised for the police that she must have taken them in a quest to kill herself. However, oddly enough, police could not locate a glass in her bedroom or bathroom that would have been used to swallow that many pills.

Her body was taken to the mortuary Sunday morning and an autopsy would discover eight mg/dL of chloral hydrate and 4.5 mg/dL of Nembutal in her system. Dr. Thomas Noguchi, of the Los Angeles County Coroners office, recorded her cause of death as "acute barbiturate poisoning," resulting from a "probable suicide." Marilyn was 36 years old. Greenson's claimed that they wanted permission from the publicity department of Twentieth Century Fox, before informing authorities, which could have accounted for the time delay. However, police questioned those at the house and the timelines began to get shaky. Police suspected others had been to the house before police were called to the scene.

Fox publicist Arthur Jacobs and two other Fox men reportedly arrived at Monroe's home in the wee hours of the morning, before police, to collect paperwork and Peter Lawford was said to have been at the house to "remove anything that might incriminate the president," according to investigator Fred Otash, who claimed Lawford had called him in to help. Monroe's lawyer, Milton Rudin, also Greenson's brother-in-law, was reportedly called to the scene before police.

While there is much mystery and innuendo about the actions and behaviors of her doctors, housekeeper and the studio, in the end, Marilyn Monroe was dead, and so was *Something's Got to Give* ... or so they thought.

sixteen

"Fame is fickle, and I know it. It has compensations but it also has draw-backs, and I've experienced them both."

- Marilyn Monroe

-

"I like joy; I want to be joyous; I want to have fun on the set; I want to wear beautiful clothes and look pretty. I want to smile and I want to make people laugh. And that's all I want. I like it. I like being happy. I want to make others happy."

- Doris Day

What Now?

With the Star Dead, Fox Ponders Its Options

If Monroe's death in the early morning hours of August 5, 1962 was a "shock" heard round the world; for Fox employees, it was only a precursor to the death blow felt little more than 24 hours later. Monday morning, August 6, at 9 a.m. more than 800 Fox employees received pink slips. A majority of the workers had been scheduled on the only film Fox had left in production in Hollywood – *Something's Got To Give*.

Executives in New York gave notice that the Hollywood sound-stages were to be vacated within 10 days and everyone was out of work. Darryl Zanuck had regained control of the studio and, within weeks, decided the only way to salvage the studio was to cancel all television and film production, lay off its employees, and screen the footage the studio had captured on *Cleopatra* to decide if they could complete the film.

When Marilyn Monroe died, estimates put her estate at $92,781. She had a balance of $1,337.53 in her City National Bank account on August 1, 1962, with an overdraft of $4,208.34 in the same account on August 3, 1962. Her account at The Irving Trust Account had a balance of $1,472.41 on August 1, 1962, but had dropped to $111.71 on August 3, 1962. Surprisingly enough, the actress had little cash on hand. Even though her name, image and work would continue to reap vast amounts of income for holders of her estate and for Fox, her actual tangible assets were far less than many would have expected.

This, in fact, would also be the case for Doris Day. While in August 1962 she considered herself a wealthy woman – as did many

around her – in reality she was being swindled out of nearly every penny she made, and amassing a debt that would nearly break her. While Day was the top female box office star, it's possible that Monroe actually may have been worth more at the time of her death than Doris Day. Both women had been victimized by male Hollywood powerbrokers controlling their careers.

Monroe's will assumed the star was worth far more money than the estate actually held. Filed for probate on August 16, 1962. Marilyn's will created a $100,000 trust for her mother's care, along with $2,500 a year for Mrs. Michael Chekhov, widow of Marilyn's acting coach. She left $10,000 to Berniece Baker Miracle, her half-sister; $10,000 to her former secretary; and $5,000 to the playwright and poet Norman Rosten, with whom Monroe had become friends during her marriage to Arthur Miller. She also left 25 percent of the estate's balance to her New York psychiatrist, Dr. Marianne Kris. The bulk of the estate, including Monroe's clothes, jewelry and other personal effects were, "to be distributed among my friends, colleagues and those to whom I am devoted." They were left in the care of Lee Strasberg.

The Strasberg bequest would ultimately bring in tens of millions of dollars from film royalties, auctions of her personal belongings, and the licensing of her image in the coming decades. In the end, a woman Monroe never really knew would earn a fortune off her death. Marilyn actually only met Lee Strasberg's third wife, Anna Mizrahi Strasberg, once. It was during an event at the United Nations, years before Paula Strasberg's death.

Marilyn's funeral became a private affair. Longtime love, ex-husband, and rumored husband-to-be, Joe DiMaggio, with permission from Marilyn's half sister, made the funeral arrangements with the help of Inez Melson, Marilyn's business manager. DiMaggio barred the Hollywood crowd from attending, making it a small funeral with close friends and those he felt had not driven Monroe to her early death. Marilyn's friend and makeup artist, Whitey Snyder, would make her look her best. Snyder said that Monroe had once said, "If anything happens, promise me you'll make me up."

Snyder said it was back during the making of *Gentlemen Prefer Blondes* that the two became close; and to ensure the promise was remembered she noted it on a gold clip, with the inscription, "While I'm Still Warm."

So, Snyder and longtime wardrobe assistant Marjorie Plecher were asked to make Marilyn glamorous one last time. They dressed her in a wig she'd worn in *The Misfits* and a simple green Pucci dress that had been a favorite of hers. She'd actually been widely photographed in the dress during her trip to Mexico a few months earlier to select furnishings for her new home.

Only 24 guests were invited to pay their respects at the service, including the Greensons, the Strasbergs, her masseur Ralph Roberts,

lawyer Milton Rudin, publicist Pat Newcomb and a core set of Marilyn's dressing-room crew. She was buried at Westwood Memorial Park. Marilyn had remarked on more than one occasion that she didn't like the idea of being buried, so DiMaggio paid $800 for a crypt and a bronze casket. The public was asked to make donations in her memory to charities that supported needy children. Fans gathered outside the gates and watched as the hearse carried her to her final resting place.

Something's Got to Give was in shambles. Fox executives found themselves down a dark hole immediately after the death of Marilyn. Her final film was clearly unfinished, and even a cursory assessment found that there was no way they could finish the film without Monroe. There were too many pivotal scenes between the actors that had yet to be filmed. While much of the backstory was there and many of scenes where Monroe was not needed had been filmed during her absence, too much was left to be shot. Monroe had filmed only one major sequence with the children; two scenes with Wally Cox; and the famous nude pool swim; but not enough was in the can to fudge the story without her.

Most of the footage captured centered on the house, aside from the opening courtroom sequence, a shoe store scene and an afternoon scene at a hotel pool. Monroe's opening scene – where she is rescued at sea – was missing; as was the honeymoon sequence and the key climax courtroom scene. Monroe's mother-in-law, played by Thelma Ritter in *Move Over, Darling,* remained to be filmed. Steve Allen did film scenes with Cyd Charisse, as her psychiatrist. Phil Silvers appeared as an insurance investigator. However, because Martin had also been sick, several of his scenes were missing. Fox had little choice but to shelve the picture.

After Dean Martin had dropped out of the picture without Monroe as his costar, Fox signed Lee Remick onto the film. If they were to re-film the picture quickly, they'd need a costar for her. They put in a call to Robert Mitchum, offering him the part of Nick Arden.

"They asked me about it, asked me to step in," Mitchum recalled years later. "But I heard from Dean and I wouldn't. She [Monroe] didn't get along with George Cukor. Cukor was foaming at the mouth. He was a basket case. I worked with him on *Desire Me*. Nobody desired any part of it."

Had Marilyn been rehired, Martin would have returned. However, without her – and with no one interested in taking the role to replace her when she was alive – it was highly unlikely anyone would want to step into her shoes so soon after her death. Fox gathered what it could of the footage from *Something's Got To Give*, and brought in a skeleton crew to begin work on a documentary on the life of Marilyn Monroe.

In an interview days after Marilyn's death, her publicist Pat Newcomb had told the press of the star's impending return to the picture,

adding mystery to her death. Since many assumed her firing could have been a strong factor in her apparent suicide, Newcomb dispelled that rumor. "Miss Newcomb attributes at least part of Marilyn's happiness during the last hours of her life to the fact that 20th Century-Fox appeared ready to resume *Something's Got to Give* with their star property again in the lead role," wrote the *Los Angeles Herald Examiner* on August 15, 1962.

Newcomb told the paper, "It pleased Marilyn very much that the picture was going back into production. And it pleased her to know that when the completed portions of the film were shown to studio executives in New York, there was a great deal of excited comment."

The immense outpouring of sadness and sympathy over the death of Fox's leading lady left the studio with one last opportunity to use the star to generate some cash. In fact, no longer having to even pay her a salary meant they could get a Monroe film after all, even without the troubled star. So, shortly after the dust settled, the studio started to cobble together a feature film documentary to pay tribute to their lost star. Simply called *Marilyn*, production began in 1962 by pulling together scenes from 15 of her most famous motion pictures and crafting an overlay of dialogue to present her life and career. Fox used only scenes from the films she made for the studio, so some of her other, more inspiring performances, like *Some Like It Hot* and *The Misfits*, were left out.

Narrated on-screen and off-screen by Doris Day's most famous co-star, Rock Hudson, the documentary premiered in April 1963 and included rare, never-before-seen footage from *Something's Got to Give*. Fans wanted to see footage of Monroe at the time of her death. So, the studio saw the documentary as a chance to make some money off the failed Cukor film and hoped enough Monroe fans would turn out to see the last captured work of Hollywood's leading sex symbol. As documentaries go, the film garnered mixed reviews, but did get some strong notices for the opportunity to see the rare unseen moments from her final film.

Without Monroe, there was little else the studio could do with the footage from *Something's Got to Give*. While Fox reportedly saved mounds of work on the film, it was merely locked into a vault where it would sit gathering dust for decades. The studio was left pondering what to do with the story and script.

Fox faced a dilemma over not only *Something's Got to Give*, but two other films were in limbo as well. *Cleopatra* was bleeding cash, and the studio was selling off everything that wasn't nailed to the floor in hopes of completing the film. Principal photography on *Cleopatra* came to a close at the end of July 1962, but lengthy post-production work had yet to be completed when Fox pulled the plug on everything.

After reviewing the Elizabeth Taylor epic, Zanuck and other studio heads knew their only chance was to complete the film and get it into theaters. Later in the year, editing and post-production work would resume on the film and *Cleopatra* would finally be released June 1963. At last, Fox could begin to recoup some of the lost money, but the $31 million price tag meant it would be some time before – or if ever the studio saw a profit.

As for Monroe, when she negotiated her return to Fox to complete *Something's Got to Give*, she signed a new contact with a hefty increase in her salary, but it was on the condition she delivered one, or possibly two pictures to the studio. Fox convinced her to begin a second film shortly after completing *Something's Got to Give*. The new film would be another comedy, but it was aimed to not only recapture the success of her past but also show her off as a more mature, worldly and successful woman – unlike the vapid blonde bombshells for which she was known. Called *I Love Louisa*, the film would surround her with a collection of Hollywood's biggest leading men. While the names were not all signed in ink, Dean Martin was again said to be one of her co-stars, along with Gene Kelly, Frank Sinatra, Robert Cummings, Dick Van Dyke and Paul Newman.

In the film, Monroe would play a glamorous, rich, and beautiful woman looking for love. While she could afford to buy anything and everything her heart desired, she was unlucky when it came to love. Every time she fell in love, before she could find her happily ever after, her new husband would die a peculiar death. Louisa would end up richer, but still searching for her one lasting true love.

Since *I Love Louisa* was in development as a script, but without any film ever being captured, Fox opted to go forward with the film. It would change the name to *What A Way to Go!* and its star would be Shirley MacLaine.

Another project that had Monroe's named tied to it was called *Goodbye Charlie*. It was a film version of George Axelrod's play, which debuted on Broadway in 1959 and starred Lauren Bacall and Sydney Chaplin. Directed by Axelrod, the play ran for 109 performances and tells the story of Charlie Sorrel, a man who is shot and killed after he is caught fooling around with another man's wife. Later, a dazed woman is found wandering on a beach. She doesn't remember much except directions to her home, the home of Charlie Sorrel.

The next morning she realizes that she is the reincarnation of Charlie. The comedy would center on Monroe's shock; and how she convinces her best friend of her identity and the humorous complications she finds herself in as she tries to make the most of her predicament. While Charlie has changed his sex, he's still a scoundrel, and eventually he gets killed again. However, when he's reincarnated again at the end of the move, he comes back as a dog.

Originally intended as a vehicle to pair Monroe with James Garner, the film would eventually be made in 1964 with Debbie Reynolds and Tony Curtis taking the starring roles.

With Fox on life support in 1963, the studio didn't have a lot of funds for major productions. Focusing on the release of *Cleopatra* was priority one, and if the documentary on Monroe could salvage some of the money spent on *Something's Got to Give*, the studio would have the money to move into production with some efforts. One cost-saving idea was to use the script from *Something's Got to Give* as a new project.

Had Fox's planned Christmas release of *Something's Got to Give* come to fruition, it would have had competition at the box office from none-other-than Doris Day. Day's competing film, *Billy Rose's Jumbo*, was released on December 21, 1962 in hopes of pulling in families looking for an escape to the movies. The musical spectacular harkened back to the turn of the century and the world of the traveling circus. It was the last musical Day would make and was released by MGM. While Day starring in a major musical seemed like a sure thing, the dated subject matter failed to ignite moviegoers, and the film suffered at the box office. Though the picture pulled in some $4 million in ticket sales and might have paid off for the studio, it cost more than $5.3 million to produce. It originally had been set for production a decade earlier, with a different cast and director; but legal issues delayed the production for years, until Day's husband, Marty Melcher, stepped into the producer's seat, claiming it as a vehicle for his wife.

However, the impending release of *Jumbo* wasn't the trigger for bringing Day on board for the reworking of *Something's Got to Give*. Day had turned down replacing Monroe before, so, the studio had to tread lightly when proposing the film. Twentieth Century Fox contacted Melcher about getting his wife to star in a picture, assuring him and his wife that the film would have a different name and an alternate script. The clincher for Melcher was that the studio wanted Day for two more films, provided the film was a hit. Melcher knew if the studio kept to the Doris Day formula, the money would come rolling in.

Fox actually saw Day as a savior to the studio due to the success of *The Thrill of It All*. What convinced them was Day's at times, not-so-subtle impersonation of Monroe. Her breathy impression of the sex goddess gave them the idea that she could pull off the sex appeal, but in doing so, remain true to her own persona. Day's screen personality was well established, and Fox had no desire to sway from that. However, seeing her fill Monroe's shoes – even for a humorous gag – gave them hope that she could help them put Marilyn Monroe behind them and create a new kind of heroine.

Fox decided they might be able to utilize not only the script and other elements of *Something's Got to Give* to develop as a vehicle for Day. Melcher agreed that as long as Day's asking price could be met and the studio could soften the script to suit Day's onscreen persona, they had a deal. While Doris Day and Marilyn Monroe may have had numerous physical similarities, Day was not the blonde bombshell – she was the girl next door.

In fact, it was the girl next door who premiered in New York City on June 14, 1962 and was a smash success in *That Touch of Mink*. Pulling in more than $8 million for Universal in its domestic release, the film was poised to head into international markets in the fall. It was raking in money as news of Marilyn Monroe's death hit headlines that August, and Fox executives wondered if they might be able to lure her to the studio with a reworking of *Something's Got to Give*.

By keeping the original story intact, Fox could make use of the existing soundstage. The replica of George Cukor's home, built on the Fox lot for Monroe, was still available and could be used to keep costs down. If they could rename the film and recast the leading lady, they might avoid the downside of Monroe's death and make the most of a difficult situation. The star was key. However, as a picture for Doris Day, they'd have to drop scenes like a nighttime skinny dip, and some other more provocative dialog, making the picture a little more light and wholesome.

Goddess & the Girl Next Door

seventeen

Goddess & the Girl Next Door

"You don't really know a person until you live with him, not just sleep with him. Sex is not enough to sustain marriage."

- Doris Day

-

"How do I know about a man's need for a sex symbol? I'm a girl."
- Marilyn Monroe

Reworking a Script.

Updating the Film to Suit a New Star

In August 1962, shortly before Monroe's death, Fox had agreed to regroup the cast and crew of *Something's Got to Give* in October to complete the film. That all changed after Monroe's death. The studio spent the next few months working on a documentary heralding Marilyn's life, including rare scenes from *Something's Got to Give*, because it was the only way they'd ever be able to use the footage.

As the last few months of 1962 came to a close, though, Fox decided they might be able to use the script and recast the leading lady. Once Marty Melcher approved the project as a vehicle for his wife, providing certain changes were made, *Something's Got to Give* would find its way back to a soundstage.

To avoid too much comparison to the ill-fated Monroe picture, Fox opted to retitle the film *Move Over, Darling*, and hired Hal Kanter and Jack Sher to rework the 1962 script by Nunnally Johnson. *The New York Times* reported that Day's version of the story would more closely resemble the earlier telling in the Cary Grant and Irene Dunne version, *My Favorite Wife*.

As the studio was preparing the release of a documentary celebrating the life of Marilyn Monroe, there was no publicity of a Doris Day project initially. The script for *Something's Got to Give* had been privately handed off to Kanter and Sher to transform it into something more suitable for Doris Day.

Hal Kanter was a writer, producer and director, whose work at the time was mostly focused on television. As a director, he'd most recently worked on *The Milton Berle Show* in 1958 and 1959, where he also filled writer and producer duties for the series.

In the early 1960s, Kanter focused on his film career, writ-

ing screenplays for MGM and Paramount Pictures. With comedy as a strength from his TV work with Berle, as well as George Gobel, Ed Wynn and Dinah Shore, Kanter crafted screenplays for Bob Hope's *Bachelor in Paradise*, Elvis Presley's *Blue Hawaii*, and Bette Davis' *Pocketful of Miracles*. Kanter's claim to fame was in writing jokes to Eddie Cantor's radio program.

Jack Sher was also a writer and director who was known for writing light comedy screenplays like *My Favorite Spy, The Kid from Left Field,* and *Love in a Goldfish Bowl.*

Kanter and Sher also had a history, having worked together in 1951 with Sher crafting the screenplay for Bob Hope's *My Favorite Spy*, while Kanter supplied additional dialog for the comedy. In 1953 they teamed up to share the screenplay duties for the comedy *Off Limits*. Starring Bob Hope and Mickey Rooney, the film also had laughs and hijinks centered on a sexy blonde. Marilyn Maxwell filled the bill, but the producers could easily have cast Monroe in the part.

Kanter later recalled that while *My Favorite Wife* was a baseline to refocus the *Something's Got To Give* script into *Move Over, Darling*,

there were other differences between the pictures. "My feeling is that in the original, when Irene [Dunne] comes back, her attitude is that this is a funny situation and she makes Cary [Grant] suffer. In this, while Doris understands there is some amusement, she suffers with him for a while and then gets damned mad."

The final version of the script for *Move Over, Darling* was completed on April 3, 1963. At about 141 pages, it would receive some reworking with about 12 blue pages of changes during production. Like *Something's Got To Give*, the story opens in a courtroom. At Los Angeles Civic Center courthouse, Judge Bryson is described as a, "cantankerous old man" who suffers from "arthritis and humanity."

Move Over, Darling kept the judge's name and characterization the same, even using some of the same lines. In both versions, Nick and Bianca are there to have Nick's first wife pronounced dead, so he can marry Bianca. In *Something's Got To Give*, Bianca distracts the judge with light bouncing off a makeup compact, while in *Move Over, Darling* the jangling of bracelets disturbs him.

For *Move Over, Darling*, Nick and Bianca head off to Monterey for a honeymoon, while the script for *Something's Got to Give* had the couple flying from San Francisco to Hawaii.

While Marilyn never filmed her return to civilization scene, Doris would film hers in early April 1963. The script was revised on April 4 describing Doris Day, turning up "at the US Navy Dock on a submarine to a great deal of hoopla, as she has returned from years lost at sea."

In *Something's Got to Give's* Nunnally Johnson script, dated March 29, 1962, the scene is described as taking place aboard a submarine. "This would be a rather close shot with the camera shooting up at the bridge from the forward deck, with the CO of the ship and another officer leaning on the rail and looking off past the camera. Then between them appears a beautiful young woman, Ellen Wagstaff Arden, who leans on the rail and looks off too. She is evidently familiar to them aboard the ship that neither of the officers gives her more than a casual notice as all three look off with smiles of anticipation at journey's end ..."

The story is explained by the ship's captain, "Don't ask me! All I know, they were taking a last look around those little islands down there before the nuclear test when they spotted this blonde waving at them from the top of a palm tree."

Though the scene was never filmed, and changed for *Move Over, Darling*, the script called for Monroe to leave the ship, "accompanied by the entire fleet of commissioned officers, one is carrying a small bundle of her belongings."

"How she is dressed will be left to the management - she is bare-footed," was noted in the script, though screen tests showed Monroe was expected to wear an outfit similar to the one worn by Doris in *Move Over, Darling*. Blue jeans and a light blue navy shirt, along with a white sailor hat would probably have been used.

"Nothing but males as far as the eye could see," according to Ellen's point of view in the script, with all the men examining her, then the officers salute her," explained the script for *Something's Got To Give*. It was planned that the rescue would drop Marilyn's character off in Hawaii, so her character would inadvertently meet up with Nick and Bianca as they arrived on their honeymoon.

In *Move Over, Darling*, Ellen is described this way. "The white hat pushed its way through the group. CLOSE ANGLE. The white hat is perched on the head of a beautiful young blonde who wears Navy denims. She is Ellen Arden, looking extremely appealing, in spite of her garb. Around her neck is a thin gold chain, with a locket at the end, tucked into her bosom. As she breaks out of the group:

SKIPPER: "Mrs. Arden: Where are you going"

ELLEN: "To a telephone: I've got to call my family."

In the original version of the script intended for *Something's Got To Give*, the script plays the scene a little differently, with Monroe being asked if there's anything the crew can do for her and she responds by asking, "I don't mean to sound as if I were complaining or anything but -

could I have a bath with the door shut?"

Monroe then asks, "Oh, for goodness sake, I completely forgot! Who's the president now?"

CAPTAIN: "Kennedy."

ELLEN: "Oh, really? Which one?" *(Had this line remained in the resulting Doris Day film it would have proved problematic with Kennedy assassinated just prior to the film's release.)*

Ellen finds a phone in the next scene in the lobby of a beach hotel. She is described similarly in both scenes, "shaking with eagerness and excitement as she waits to speak to her family. She can hear the phone ringing."

In *Something's Got To Give*, Ellen is calling from Hawaii when she speaks to her son, Timmy, for the first time. He doesn't remember her, only saying his, "Mommy is dead," and that he has a new mother. "We've got a new Mommy now," he tells her.

ELLEN: "What do you mean, you've got a new Mommy?"

TIMMY: "Bianca, Daddy says she's our new Mommy."

ELLEN: "When?"

TIMMY: "Today."

ELLEN: "Where are they now - Daddy and this new Mommy?"

TIMMY: "They went away in a plane."

In the reworking for *Move Over, Darling*, Kanter and Sher decide to ditch the plane trip honeymoon and Hawaii locale, opting to keep Ellen closer to Los Angeles. Ellen, this time, is unable to reach her family, because the phone number has been changed. She asks for a nickel, but phone calls now cost a dime, and after dialing she finds the number inactive and changed. She doesn't have a pencil to write down the new number and can't remember all the digits; so she gives up on the call and decides to head directly to the house, not learning until later from her mother-in-law that her husband has remarried.

While the general story remained true in the reworking, *Move Over, Darling*, lost any racy dialogue and jettisoned the sexier side of the leading lady. Day would certainly not submit to a nude scene, and the dream sequence of her on a deserted island with a man other than her husband would have to be played for laughs rather than sex appeal. While fans would have expected Monroe to show off her figure, Doris Day required a far more wholesome characterization of Ellen Arden.

Day and Melcher approved the rewrites and production began shortly after the script was completed. While Fox would be a year late, this time they hoped for a Christmas 1963 release.

eighteen

Goddess & the Girl Next Door

"What a tragedy it is for a couple to get married, have a child, and in the process discover they are not suited for one another!"

- Doris Day

-

"I think when you're famous, every weakness is exaggerated."

- Marilyn Monroe

Doris to the Rescue.

Fox Regroups and Signs Doris Day to Finish Their Movie

As Master of Ceremonies for the annual Hollywood Foreign Press Association's 19th Dinner on March 5, 1962, Rock Hudson had the chance to share the stage with both Marilyn Monroe and Doris Day.

235

While he and Day were now longtime friends, having worked on several
films, Marilyn Monroe was someone he would never work alongside.

However, that evening in March, Hudson presented Monroe with
a Golden Globe award for World Favorite Female actress of the year.
Monroe hadn't won the award for any specific film, but rather for her
stardom and body of work. Hudson and Monroe posed for pictures for
the press and made newspapers around the world. She had won the same
award in 1954, along with a Golden Globe for Best Actress in 1959.
Little did Hudson know that months later he would be narrating a documentary on her life, eulogizing the star, shortly after her tragic death.

Marilyn, the documentary, was released in April 1963 to mixed
reviews. Chronicling her life through the Fox films she made, the film
contained the only clips from *Something's Got To Give* that Fox cobbled
together. For nearly three decades, it was the only footage the public ever
saw of Monroe's uncompleted film. The studio had roughly 20 minutes
of usable footage and because the film couldn't be completed without
her, Fox executives saw the documentary as a chance to use the little
footage they had of Monroe's last movie to recoup some of the money
they had spent.

By the time the documentary was released on April 18, 1963, nearly every Monroe film had been re-released in theater chains around the country. In the months after her death, fans were eager to revisit the films that made her a movie star, and Fox had a chance to once again make money off Marilyn Monroe. *Marilyn* became the first documentary film to ever hit the top 20 box office hits in its initial release.

While Monroe's footage from *Something's Got to Give* had little use for the studio, Fox had held onto the sets on Soundstage 14, looking to get some return on its investment in its failed film. Since there were no productions requiring the use of the Fox soundstage, sets for the family home and portions of the elaborate island dream sequence could be utilized in early 1963 for *Move Over, Darling*. While Cukor would be out as director, the replica of his house and pool would remain.

Though Doris refused to replace Marilyn on *Something's Got to Give*, her husband convinced her that the new film would be an entirely different project. With a new name and a reworked script, Marty Melcher saw the project as another wholesome comedy that would keep Day's squeaky-clean persona intact. Gone were the implied adultery, suggestive banter and blatant sex appeal of the Monroe picture. In place of it, moviegoers would get mom, apple pie, and hopefully lots of laughter.

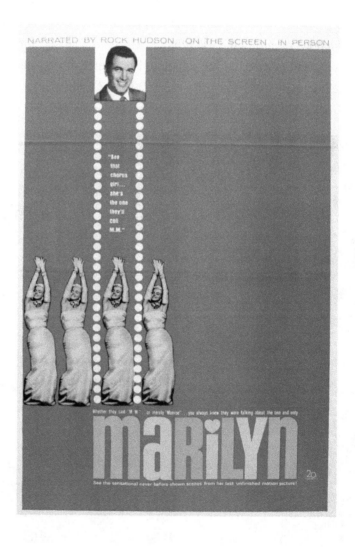

Marty Melcher kept a tight reign on Doris' acting and musical career and saw to it her onscreen persona remained every bit the girl next door. Melcher had been overseeing to Day's career for a long time.

The two met in 1947 when Day's music career was taking off. Doris was being represented by Al Levy of Century Artists. Levy recognized Day's obvious vocal talent, as well as her potential as a movie star when no one else did. With her second marriage to saxophonist George Weidler coming to an end in late 1946 – only eight months after the wedding – Levy began escorting Day to Hollywood parties to introduce her to the right people in the business. It was on one such evening when she met Director Michael Curtiz who offered Doris her first film role, *Romance on the High Seas*. Once her career was launched, Levy saw a

bright future, but so did Marty Melcher. Melcher was one of Levy's partners at Century Artists. He happened to be married to Patty Andrews of The Andrew Sisters singing group. After Melcher met Doris, he quickly saw a star he could latch onto and began escorting Day around town. Soon the two were having an affair, and he would begin representing her. After his divorce from Andrews in 1950, he proposed to Day and the two married on her birthday on April 3, 1951.

Doris moved artist representation from Levy to Melcher. By the time they were married every career decision was being made by her husband. He was selecting her projects and negotiating her salary. He would ultimately manage all her finances, and she would pay a costly price for it.

By 1962, the Melcher marriage was on the rocks, and it was more of a professional partnership than a union of man and wife. Even through adultery, mistrust and his bad treatment of her son, she continued to let him manage her career and empire. When the two considered divorce in 1962, she never sought anyone else to handle her career. It had been reported that the pressure to maintain her success put a strain on the marriage and by the early 1960s, they acted more like business associates than a couple. Melcher had convinced her that divorce could ruin her financially. They put their divorce plans aside, but stopped sleeping together. They remained cordial with each other, but the romance was gone.

In announcing the picture, Melcher told the press not to expect nude shots by the swimming pool like the "much-publicized ones" of Monroe. In describing the reworked version he said, "It will be sort of a married *Pillow Talk* ... what we call 'clean sex.'"

If her love life was nothing to write home about, her career was still stellar, and she was at the top of her game. With *Move Over, Darling*, Day's Ellen Arden would dress every bit as glamorous as Monroe's. Though Jean Louis would be gone, Moss Mabry, would keep Day looking stylish, yet approachable. Mabry had dressed Natalie Wood in *Rebel*

Without a Cause, Elizabeth Taylor in *Giant*, and Janet Leigh in *Manchurian Candidate*. He had been under contract for Warner Bros. for years, and this film would be his first project under a new deal with Fox.

For his first outing with Doris Day, Mabry had to dress Day down early on in the film when she's rescued at sea; but he had the costume plans from *Something's Got to Give* to go on. Similar to Monroe's costume, Day would wear sailor's clothes, including blue jeans and a sailor hat, but as the film progressed she would dress in stylish suits and dresses. Mabry would also be tasked with dressing the other Mrs. Arden. This time, instead of Cyd Charisse, the role went to another artist once represented by Marty Melcher, Polly Bergen. Bergen didn't get the role through Melcher; however, it was the director who wanted her in the part.

"I had, at that point, only starred in films, and I said, 'well, I don't want to play second banana to Doris Day' who was the biggest star in the world and has got to be a complete and total pain in the neck." recalled Bergen. "[S]he'll arrive at noon to be photographed. They'll be shooting me at six in the morning and the camera will never be on me in a shot that she's in – it'll be, you know, on the back of my head, on her, and I'm not going to do this movie."

However, Director Michael Gordon refused to take no for an answer, convinced the part was perfect for her. Gordon had directed Bergen in the Broadway production of "Champagne Complex" at the Cort Theater in April 1955. Eventually convinced to take the role, Bergen never regretted her decision. "I so fell in love with her [Doris]. She was the most wonderful, funny, delicious, completely sharing, giving actress I had ever worked with – and I mean that sincerely."

Other key supporting roles were also recast, including Ellen's fellow castaway and rival for her husband, Stephen Burkett, also known as "Adam" to Ellen's "Eve" in the both films. Tom Tryon was recast for this outing with Chuck Connors, who was just coming off his successful run on TV as *The Rifleman*. Don Knotts would replace Wally Cox as the shoe salesman Ellen persuades to pretend to be her "Adam," and comedy actor Edgar Buchanan would take on the role of Judge Bryson, formerly played by John McGiver in the Monroe version. Other appearances by Fred Clark, John Astin, Pat Harrington and Elliott Reid would fill out smaller roles. The Arden children would be recast as well.

In addition to Thelma Ritter, several other *Move Over, Darling* cast members had a history working with Marilyn Monroe. Fred Clark appeared as a hotel clerk in the film and had worked with Monroe in *How to Marry a Millionaire* in 1953. Elliott Reid also had worked with Monroe in 1953, in *Gentlemen Prefer Blondes*. He would appear opposite Day as Dr. Herman Schlick with most of his scenes opposite Polly Bergen.

In part to cut costs and to ease location shooting for the stars, the opening sequences for *Something's Got to Give*, which were originally

set in Hawaii, reverted to Los Angeles for *Move Over, Darling.*

The opening courtroom scene and rescue at sea were fundamentally unchanged except for minor adjustments. In the courtroom, rather than distracting the judge with a reflection of light from her makeup compact, Bianca's noisy bracelets disturb him. For the return to civilization, the scenes are similar, except Monroe's sexy exit that grabbed the attention of the sailors. Day's exit comes off more as one of the boys. In both pictures, Ellen telephones home, but only in the Monroe version does she get through. In *Move Over, Darling*, Ellen has trouble finding the phone number and opts to go directly home to find her family in person.

For the honeymoon, the flight to Hawaii is replaced with Nick and Bianca driving up the coast from Los Angeles to Monterey. Instead of arriving at the hotel, Day arrives at home and encounters her mother-in-law, played by Thelma Ritter. It's been suggested that Ritter was a likely choice for the same role in *Something's Got To Give*, but the part was never filmed. In the reworking, Day learns her husband has remarried and is off on his honeymoon. She's encouraged to get to Monterey before they consummate the marriage and to reunite with her husband.

Nailing down the part of Nick Arden was easy. Fox saw her co-star James Garner, from *The Thrill of It All* as the perfect replacement for Dean Martin. The chemistry between Day and Garner showed onscreen, and the success of their earlier film meant built in audience appeal. In addition, he was cheaper than Rock Hudson and had been Fox's original choice for leading man in *Something's Got to Give.*

Goddess & the Girl Next Door

nineteen

"If I had lived with Al Jorden for a few weeks, God knows I would never have married him. Nor would I have married George Weidler. But I was too young and too inexperienced to understand any of this. Now my heart was busted and I had lost my way."

- Doris Day

"Marriage destroyed my relationship with two wonderful men."
- Marilyn Monroe

A Leading Man.

James Garner Re-Teams with Day In Hopes of a Hit

Dean Martin had met Doris Day back around 1953 at a charitable event for children. Martin was an emcee that evening, walking around encouraging people to sing. When he saw Doris he immediately recruited her to entertain the crowd with a song. Doris hated being asked to sing on the spot, but at Dean's urging, and not wanting to let people down at the fundraiser, Doris agreed. However, for years after, she refused to attend the charitable event. She never forgot Dean Martin for having put her on the spot.

By the time *Move Over, Darling* was underway, Dean Martin had long since moved on. After having rejected Fox's request that he complete *Something's Got To Give* with another actress, it was unlikely he would be willing to star opposite Doris Day in the reworking of the script. However, Fox never really considered him, opting to go with a more familiar Day co-star.

James Garner had a non-speaking part in the Broadway production of *The Caine Mutiny Court-Martial* in 1954, where he shared the stage with Henry Fonda. Night after night, he studied Fonda and by the end of the run he'd decided to focus on acting as a career. He'd come a long way.

Born James Scott Bumgarner on April 7, 1928 in Norman, Okla-

homa, he was the youngest of three sons. After his mother died when he was five-years-old, the boys were sent to live with relatives. When his father remarried about a year later, the boys returned to live with their father and his new bride.

Garner despised his stepmother, because she beat her stepsons. When he was 14, she left her husband and sons. The boys were now becoming men and were too big to abuse. At 16, James joined the United States Merchant Marines. At the end of World War II he returned home and met up with his father, who was now living in Los Angeles. He enrolled at Hollywood High School. After graduating, he enlisted in the National Guard, serving in Korea for 14 months as a rifleman during the Korean War. He was wounded twice and received the Purple Heart.

After his brief stint on Broadway, Garner found work in television, first in commercials and then in TV shows. His first film roles were in 1956 in T*he Girl He Left Behind* and *Toward the Unknown*.

In 1957, he changed his last name from Bumgarner to Garner after the studio had credited him as "James Garner." It wasn't long after that he landed the role that would make him famous. As Bret Maverick in *Maverick*, Garner became known to TV western fans for three seasons. He also appeared in one episode of the fourth season, but by then he was becoming a movie star, opposite Doris Day.

After roles in *The Children's Hour* and *Boys' Night Out* in 1962, he was cast in *The Thrill of It All*. After his leading man role in *Move Over, Darling* in 1963, theater exhibitors voted him the 16th most popular star in the United States.

Garner quickly became a fan of Day, and the feeling was mutual. "I think Doris is a very sexy lady who doesn't know how sexy she is," he once said. "That's an integral part of her charm. One other thing about acting with Doris – she was the Fred Astaire of comedy. Whether it was Rock Hudson or Rod Taylor or me, or whoever – we all looked good because we were all dancing with Clara Bixby. ... Making a moving with Doris was a piece of cake."

Universal's *The Thrill of It All* would be released in July 1963, and all indications were that the film was a surefire hit. It was clear that the chemistry between Garner and Day elevated the slapstick comedy with witty banter and a romantic flair that audiences were looking for. Re-teaming the duo for *Move Over, Darling* could capitalize on the on-screen chemistry if the film were a hit. While Day would deliver her

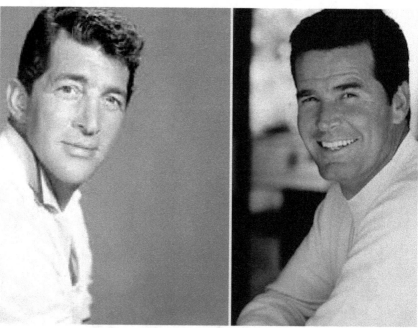

usual antics and wholesome charm, Garner balanced her with an exasper-ated despair. Unlike Rock Hudson's sly trickery and deception that was often present in his outings with Day, Garner played second fiddle to Day's star, allowing her charm to ooze off the screen, much in the same way Desi Arnaz backed Lucille Ball in *I Love Lucy.*

One person Garner was not fond of was her husband, Marty Melcher. "Marty was a hustler, a shallow, insecure hustler who always ripped off $50,000 on every one of Doris' films as a price for making the deal," he said. "When we were making *Move Over, Darling* he was bragging a lot about money he had just borrowed from the Teamsters to finance some big hotel or other. A wheeler-dealer businessman, but of course, we all knew where his clout came from and without Doris he couldn't have driven a truck for the Teamsters. I never knew anyone who liked Melcher."

Key to pulling off the second teaming of Day and Garner would be the director. While Fox wanted to build on the pre-existing chemistry, the story had to stand on its own, and put space and distance from the originally-planned *Something's Got to Give.* Michael Gordon was the man for the job.

Born Irving Kunin Gordon in 1909, Michael Gordon was first an American stage actor before his career as a director took hold. He was a member of the Group Theatre from 1935 until 1940. When a career as an actor seemed unlikely, Gordon took a stab at directing, first with a short film, *A Short Landfall,* in 1941, and then his first feature, *Boston Blackie Goes Hollywood,* in 1942.

He would work regularly through the 1940s with a series of films, including *Crime Doctor* in 1943, *The Web* in 1947, *Another Part of the Forest* and *An Act of Murder,* both in 1948, and *The Lady Gambles* and *Once More, My Darling,* both in 1949. The 1950s started off prom-ising with *Cyrano de Bergerac* in 1950, *I Can Get It for You Wholesale,* and *The Secret of Convict Lake,* both in 1951.

Around 1951, Gordon's career hit a roadblock when he was

blacklisted as a Communist. Senator Joseph McCarthy's hunt for communists accused Gordon of communist leanings after it was learned he had early affiliation with some leftist organizations. He found himself blacklisted and unable to find work in the United States. After making one film in Australia, Gordon returned to the U.S. and joined the faculty of the UCLA Theater Department. He also spent summers at Pine Brook Country Club Group Theatre in Connecticut. A number of artists like Elia Kazan, Harry Morgan, John Garfield, Lee J. Cobb, Will Geer, Clifford Odets, Howard Da Silva and Irwin Shaw, some of which also felt the sting of the blacklist, spent time there.

He returned to Hollywood after producer Ross Hunter hired him to direct Doris Day and Rock Hudson in *Pillow Talk*. He would work for Hunter again in 1960's *Portrait in Black*, starring Lana Turner, and then in 1962 he would direct *Boys' Night Out*, starring Kim Novak.

"Comedy is the most serious tragedy in the world," he once said. "Play it that way and you can't go wrong. If you ever think of yourself as funny, you haven't got a chance."

In 1963, Gordon would direct *For Love and Money*, starring Mitzi Gaynor. He would be called back to duty for Doris Day, when Fox hired him to direct *Move Over, Darling*. The success of *Pillow Talk* was the driving force behind hiring Gordon. The box office success and reviews gave Fox hope that Gordon could make the most of the story and the Day-Garner pairing would bring the fans to the theater.

twenty

"I'm afraid it's going to shock some people for me to say this, but I staunchly believe no two people should get married until they have lived together. The young people have it right."

- Doris Day

-

"I think one of the basic reasons men make good friends is that they can make their minds up quickly."

- Marilyn Monroe

Move Over.

A New Set of Stars Take Over A Familar Tale

The pairing of Doris Day and James Garner, in fact, would provide Fox with established familiarity, with this being their second onscreen teaming. Having starred in *The Thrill of it All,* released in July

1963, the film would become one of the highest grossing films of the year, making both stars strong box office draws. It would stand to reason that a reteaming of the duo could breathe new life into the failed Monroe film and help fans forget about the former star's association with the story.

Fox's ability to repackage the story, renaming it and casting the biggest female box office star of the day would be a smart move for a studio in the hole financially. *The Thrill of it All* pulled in nearly $11.8 million for Universal-International, making it a profitable venture for the studio. If Fox could capture that success, it might salvage the studio.

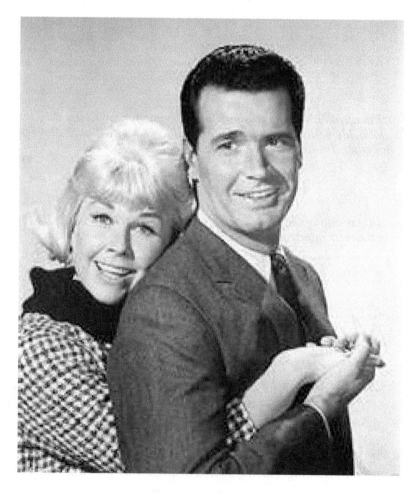

Of *The Thrill of It All, Variety* said, "Doris Day scores as the housewife," and *The New York Times* wrote, "Doris Day has finally got back to having a husband and some kids and is acting her age in her latest knockabout comedy."

Fox figured the established chemistry between Day and Garner would help audiences revisit *The Thrill of It All* and put distance between the bad publicity surrounding *Something's Got to Give*. The humor of the old married couple was established by the earlier teaming of Day and Garner, and the humor could be more family forward and less suggestive, as the Monroe script implied. One pivotal scene in the picture that required finesse was the moment Ellen and Nick meet again for the first time and he realizes his dead wife is in fact alive.

In *Something's Got to Give*, the final script dated March 29, 1962, left some of the never-filmed scene open to the director, explaining:

"Seated on the floor, Ellen is still pondering what would seem to be an insoluble problem. And now a suggestion for the director, because the movements involved must be governed by the arrangement of the set. Nick and Ellen pass each other two or three times ... She goes to buy a newspaper, he crosses to get cigarettes, etc. But five years have passed since they last saw each other, and Nick doesn't even know she is alive. Even a murmured "Pardon me" might follow a close miss. This is when one longs for an old-time gag man - held under tight rein, of course. It is a situation worth plotting out on the set."

The meeting takes place when "They follow the baggage across the lobby to the elevator, and he follows them and this time when they pass, Ellen she happens to be looking directly at Nick. Recognition to her slowly and not all surely. Am I crazy? Is it - just a remarkable resemblance? She is still a thousand miles from certain when they enter the elevator and turn to face the still open door and for the first time their eyes meet. It IS him! It is! As for Nick, he is seeing a ghost/ His chin drops and his knees turn to water. The operator closes the door."

Nick and Bianca are in the elevator as the door closes, while Ellen remains in the lobby. Both are stunned.

Nick's face is still that of a corpse, of a man who died of fright.

BIANCA: "What's the matter, darling?"

He doesn't answer. He can't. The denial hasn't stuck.

Ellen, now angry that her husband has seen her and is off with his new wife, rents a hotel suite and looks to buy new clothes, all charging it to his bill. She also sends up a bottle of champagne to the happy couple with a note.

When Nick get's champagne with the note, it reads, "From yours forever, Ellen - remember?"

In *Move Over, Darling* the script offered a similar but abbreviated encounter in the lobby of the hotel in Monterey, having Ellen encountering Nick and Bianca, but not saying anything. Then, as the elevator

door closes Nick and Ellen lock eyes. Bianca fails to notice her husband's dilemma. A bottle of champagne is again sent to Nick and Bianca, but instead of a note with the delivery, the script called for the locket, seen earlier around Ellen's neck, which falls out of an envelope into Nick's hand. The bellboy then tells Nick, the delivery is from a woman waiting downstairs.

The scripts held very similar stories and scenes, though some scenes were adjusted in *Move Over, Darling* to downplay sex and adultery.

Both scripts have similar meetings between Ellen and Nick, with their discussing her funeral with 200 guests and a coffin covered in pink carnations. Both are shocked – one to find that his dead wife is in fact alive, and the other that her husband has a new wife.

In *Something's Got to Give*, Nick's inability to consummate his new marriage leaves Bianca feeling he needs psychiatric care, and the couple agree to head back home for help from Bianca's doctor. Nick has learned that Ellen has left as well. In *Move over, Darling*, Nick fakes a back injury to avoid his marital night with Bianca, and the two head home early.

Ellen arrives in San Francisco and returns to the Arden home in *Something's Got to Give*, meeting her children for the first time since her disappearance. The scene is similar to the scene with Day in *Move Over, Darling*, except it comes earlier in the film, before she heads off to stop the honeymoon. The location is also changed to Los Angeles.

In *Something's Got to Give*, Ellen takes on the role of a children's nurse to gain entry to the house under Bianca's unknowing eyes. A similar series of scenes occur in *Move Over, Darling*, with Ellen pretending to be a Swedish nurse hired for Nick's fake back injury. The only difference seems to be that in *Something's Got to Give*, she calls herself Ms. Ingrid Tic, while in *Move Over, Darling* she's named Ms. Swenson.

In *Something's Got to Give*, Ellen returns to the home in the evening to find her two children in her bed. "You didn't drown, did you

Mommy?"

It's this important scene that Monroe's character realizes her children now remember her after finding her in an old photo with their father. The scene varies in *Move Over, Darling* with the children not telling Ellen they remember her until the end of the picture.

The latter part of the script of *Move Over, Darling* was altered on April 5, 1963 in the scene leading up to the realization that Nick hasn't met the man with whom Ellen was stranded on the desert island. It's her mother in law, played by Thelma Ritter, who suggests she find a more "suitable" man, one that is "less threatening."

However, both films have similar scenes with men arriving at the house, charging him with bigamy as the secrets begin to unravel.

Avoiding the sex appeal from Monroe's film, the script for *Move Over, Darling* required dropping several scenes and inserting more slapstick humor, including a Swedish massage that turns into a brawl between Ellen and Bianca.

In one dropped scene from *Something's Got to Give*, Monroe

steps out of her nurse's uniform, wearing a bathing suit underneath and she gets into the pool with the children. She then engages with Nick during the scene, as she continues to pretend to be Ms. Tic, since the children are still not aware she is their long-dead mother. In *Move Over, Darling,* Day is not seen in a bathing suit, except for the jungle cover-up that suffices for one in the elaborate dream sequence that shows little of her figure. Day is filmed wearing a blue two-piece that has artificial vines and large flowers sewn to it that bind the top and the bottom and eliminated much of sexiness from the scene.

While *Move Over, Darling* is far more wholesome, *Something's Got to Give* has Nick and Ellen more engaged. "Ellen and Nick are in each other's arms, clinging desperately to each other in the face of the situation before them," writes one scene in the script. Then later, "They kiss, though not as much as he would have liked, for even in her melting mood, she is not yet prepared to lose all that control. So, withdrawing her lips, she resumes her cuddling without really yielding. Nick looks around helplessly. She is soft and warm in his arms, and the fragrance of her hair is making him a little dizzy."

For *Move Over, Darling,* the scenes are played more for laughs, as Bianca tries to get Nick into bed, and Ellen finds ways to distract and guilt him away from her. Monroe engages in little physical comedy in her version, with most of the physical acts more subtle. She tends to prefer going barefoot, kicking off her shoes in various scenes. She also is found climbing trees and sitting on the ground, because those actions feel comfortable to her, having been stranded for so long. This is dropped in Day's version. In *Move Over, Darling,* the subtlety of the performance is lost with more comedic moments. In fact, both films featured an elaborate dream sequence; but in *Something's Got to Give* the scene was never filmed and the studio was considering dropping it to save money, even though found in the final script.

Monroe's Ellen leaves with the children later in the film, while Day's Ellen never does. After Nick is accused of bigamy and the cast of characters head back to court, a similar sequence of events takes place to bring the film to a close. Bianca wants and annulment, while Ellen wants her legally dead status reversed. Nick looks to defend his bigamy charges with the fact that he didn't know his first wife was still alive and that his first wife was declared legally dead at the time of his second wedding.

Scenes between Ellen, Nick and "Adam" – her companion on the deserted island – differ slightly, but the premise is the same. Dr. Travers in *Something's Got To Give*, becomes Dr. Herman Schlick in *Move Over, Darling*. The confusion between the handsome Adam and the fake Adam remains. Nick's jealousy, envisioning Burkett and Ellen as Adam and Eve stranded together, creates tension in both films. In *Something's Got to Give,* the sexual tension between Monroe and her supposed island lover might have played out more seriously. While Monroe was more scantily clad in two-piece swimsuits in costume fittings, Day's entire midsection is covered by a swimsuit supposedly made of island flower and fauna, with little of her figure on display. Since the island dream sequence was never filmed in *Something's Got to Give*, one will never know how Monroe might have filmed the scene, but Doris Day's version is clearly played for humor and limited sexual innuendo.

twenty-one

Goddess & the Girl Next Door

"I have the unfortunate reputation of being Miss Goody Two-shoes, America's Virgin, and all that ..."

- Doris Day

-

"I'm one of the world's most self-conscious people. I really have to struggle."

- Marilyn Monroe

Film & Release.

The Completed Film At Last Finds Its Way to Movie Screens in Late 1963

Filming on *Move Over, Darling* was set to begin on April 1, 1963, but was delayed several weeks due to James Garner's availability. Garner was completing *The Wheeler Dealers* for MGM. Playing a Texas tycoon, Garner stars in the romantic comedy which would be released shortly before his Doris Day picture. Ironically, his costar was Lee Remick, the original actress hired to replace Marilyn Monroe in *Something's Got to Give*.

When filming did begin in mid-April, the cast and director were familiar with one another, and production kicked off smoothly with the usual camaraderie of Day's last few romantic comedy outings. However, Doris Day continued to have concerns about her appearance. According to one of the publicists on the set, on several occasions Day would request that the cameraman be replaced when she didn't feel she was being captured at her best.

Early in production, one key laugh scene got out of control. In a new scene not found in *Something's Got to Give*, a frustrated Nick picks Ellen up and dramatically carries her out of the room and away from confrontation with Bianca. The scene went slightly awry when Garner got carried away. "She was standing on a bed, and I reached up, grabbed her by the waist and carried her off," recalled Garner. "In the process, I broke two of her ribs. I didn't know it until one of the assistant directors told me the next day, because Doris never complained."

The Los Angeles Times reported that Day's physician, Dr. Frederick Ilfeld tended to the star and found she suffered a cracked rib. "She will have to wear an elastic brace for four weeks, but will be able to finish the picture," the newspaper reported.

Doris returned to work after a few days off to recuperate, saying later that for the remainder of production, she was "mummified with adhesive tape" around her ribcage. Between takes she would return to her dressing room to rest and catch her breath.

On the upside, Day's spirits were boosted by one of two on-set publicists hired for the film. Fox reportedly brought in the second publicist not for his public relations skills, but in hopes of keeping Doris Day from worrying about her looks on camera. The man, known as a sports enthusiast, memorized batting averages for every player on the Los Angeles Dodgers. Since Doris was such a big fan of the team and baseball in general, the two could talk about baseball between takes and she would keep her mind off of shooting or how she was coming off on camera.

Day's love of baseball caused a bit of trouble during the filming of the department store scene with Don Knotts, when the sound operators became perplexed by troubling buzz that was being picked up by the recording equipment on the set. It was soon discovered that Doris was hiding a small transistor radio in her costume so she could listen to the World Series.

The cast clicked well, and things ran smoothly. The director credited Day for a large portion of that. Michael Gordon said, "One of the things I remember with pleasure and admiration is the unswerving dedication to truth that characterized her approach to comedy. It was her own unique comedic truth, to be sure, but it was comparable in its own terms to what she was able to draw on so movingly in films like *The Man Who Knew Too Much* and *Midnight Lace*."

As the shooting neared completion, there was still one key sequence left to capture on film. It was a new scene, not included in either the original *My Favorite Wife* or the reworked *Something's Got to Give*. For the climax of the picture, Ellen attempts to escape her husband and goes on the run. She finds refuge in a car wash and hides inside one of the vehicles on route to be cleaned, only to find herself being washed out

as well. After she accidentally releases the car's convertible roof during the trip through the machine, she's pounded by soap foam and water, much to the amusement of the audience.

The director scheduled the big scene for the last day of production because production, staff were concerned that chemicals in the detergent might affect Day's complexion. Fortunately, the scene went off without a hitch. They later confessed their worries to Day and used the item in promotional material for the film.

Gordon recalled that Doris contributed a vital ad-lib to the scene. "Visualize Doris trapped in a convertible with the top down, doused with detergent foam and drenched with spray. Then suddenly as the terrifying revolving cylinder of brushes is inexorably bearing down on her, over the horrendous dim you hear her cry out faintly, in poignant desperation, 'My hair!' The screenwriters and I wished we'd thought of something like that. Doris spontaneously did – frequently."

After 53 days, shooting of *Move Over, Darling* ended in late June. One of the additions to a Doris Day film was the opportunity to have her record a catchy pop tune for the opening credits that might also find its way to the radio and record sales, creating another opportunity to promote from the film and profit from the star's talents. *Move Over, Darling* was no exception.

A pop tune by Joe Lubin was penned for Doris to record, but the production code office took issue with the lyrics. Lubin wrote three songs for Days 1959 film *Teacher's Pet* and composed for her again for *Please Don't Eat the Daisies* (1960). Their successful collaborations would lead to his hire as vice-president of the Doris Day-Marty Melcher Music Publishing Company. His lyrics to *Move Over, Darling*, however, caused concern with suggestive lyrics like:

"Oh I yearn to be kissed – Move over darling."

"How can I resist – move over darling."

"Come into my arms and be more than just company to me – Make love to me."

Lubin was asked to adjust the lyrics to make it less suggestive. After several days collaborating with screenwriter Hal Kantor, he'd come up with a suitable alternative:

"You've captured by heart."

"And now that I'm no longer free – Please treat me tenderly"

"Move over darling – make love to me."

When the song was actually recorded, Doris' son Terry became instrumental in completing the pop tune. Terry was a young music producer and had been helping his mother create a more modern 1960s pop sound. "They'd brought me the song for the film, and I didn't think it was so great. I said we can do this title, but I'll have to rewrite the thing."

However, Day's husband Marty was less enthusiastic about updating Doris' sound for the new pop and rock and roll hitting radio airwaves. Like her onscreen persona, he fought to keep Doris grounded in the wholesome styles to which her fans had grown accustomed. In the end, it would also be a costly move and as the 60s wore on, Day became less and less relevant in the music industry, and she would drop off the pop charts dramatically.

By December, the film was ready to open nationwide. Fox's promotion of the movie avoided connections to Monroe's failed *Something's Got to Give,* focusing rather on the reteaming of Day and Garner. "Doris Day, long on the Top Ten player list in Box-office barometer, and James Garner, rapidly climbing to popularity through *The Great Escape* and *The Thrill of it All,* the latter another co-starring role with Miss Day, which became one of the smash hits of 1963, now appear in another madcap comedy which is certain to repeat in audience appeal and the resultant sensational box-office generally," said one promotional piece.

Released on Christmas Day 1963, the comedy was a much-needed boost for American audiences who were still dealing with the assassination of President John F. Kennedy, only a month earlier. Oddly enough, Doris had her own historic tie to the Kennedy assassination when she recently had just become owner of The Cabana Motor Hotel in Dallas. Sitting on the Stemmons Freeway, the hotel was mainly an investment for Doris – arranged by her husband – but the location had a front seat for the tragic events that day as Kennedy's motorcade sped

by on its way to the hospital. She would sell the hotel to Hyatt House in 1969.

With a budget of $3,350,000, Fox was convinced they had a hit on their hands with *Move Over, Darling*, and recouping their costs with Day and Garner on the screen would be easy. They would be right.

With a box office take of roughly $6 million in North America alone, the studio recouped their costs quickly and went into the black.

An estimated additional $7 million from the international release in 1964 helped make the film one of the top romantic comedies of the year. While *Cleopatra* was the number one box office hit of the year, pulling in roughly $26 million in U.S. rentals, at a cost of nearly $38 million meant the film would take years to return its investment to the studio. *Move Over, Darling*, on the other hand, was the only other Fox hit that year, and immediately provided cash back to the studio.

Motion Picture Magazine called the film, "One of the funniest, brightest marital adventures of the year, Day and Garner are superb in predicaments that are hilarious" and *BBC Radio Times* said, "This film shows how her [Doris Day's] great talent has endured. Slick, utterly professional and without a wasted scene, this is sheer delight from start to finish."

Variety offered a mixed bag in their review, writing, "Doris Day and James Garner play it to the hilt, comically, dramatically and last, but not least (particularly in the case of the former), athletically. What is missing in their portrayals is a light touch - the ability to humorously convey with a subtle eyelash-bat or eyebrow-arch what it tends to take

them a kick in the shins to accomplish."

Not everyone missed the ties to *Something's Got to Give*. *The New York Times* noted the reworking in a December article, writing, "For the record, it should be noted that *My Favorite Wife* was being remade, and scrapped, last year as *Something's Got to Give*, starring the late Marilyn Monroe. Essentially, however, it is still the screwy saga of a man who remarries, thinking his wife is dead, and the wacky involvements that follow when the first wife turns up just as he is about to start on his honeymoon. With or without comparisons with the original, however, *Move Over, Darling* appears to be straining and shouting for effects that should be natural and uncontrived."

However, when the awards season came around, Day once again found herself recognized with a Golden Globe nomination for Best Actress in a Comedy or Musical, though she would lose the award to Shirley MacLaine for *Irma la Douce*.

Fox was so happy with their use of Doris Day that they negotiated to have her make two more films for the studio. While Day was flush with film projects, Melcher took the money; and Day would return to Fox to make *Do Not Disturb*, released in 1965, and *Caprice*, released in 1967.

twenty-two

"I believe that everything happens for a reason. People change so that you can learn to let go, things go wrong so that you appreciate them when they're right, you believe lies so you eventually learn to trust no one but yourself, and sometimes good things fall apart so better things can fall together."

- Marilyn Monroe

-

"I'm a difficult character to live with."

- Doris Day

What remains.

Film historian Sam Wasson wrote in his book *Fifth Avenue, 5 AM*, that in the late 1950s and early 60s, leading ladies traditionally fell into two camps. "For women in movies, there existed an extreme dialectic. On the one end there was Doris Day, and on the other, Marilyn Monroe."

If Monroe and Day were opposing forces in Hollywood, it was Hollywood's own doing – having created the immensely popular and powerful personas of Marilyn Monroe and Doris Day. For the actresses, the onscreen personalities that characterized them would present them with major challenges in sustaining lasting careers.

By most accounts, in the final days of her life, Marilyn Monroe was focused on her future and building a career that would sustain her. She had a host of film projects in the works. Arrangements had been made to return to complete *Something's Got to Give*; and the studio had a number of other features with her name penciled to them. In addition to the earlier mentioned *What A Way To Go!* and *Goodbye Charlie*, Monroe was considered the strongest contender to star as an insecure and aging showgirl in a drama tentatively titled "Woman of Summer." The film would eventually be made with Joanne Woodward and released in 1963 under the title, *The Stripper. What a Way to Go!* would release in 1964

with Shirley MacLaine and *Goodbye Charlie* would star Debbie Reynolds in 1965.

Monroe also had parts lined up elsewhere. Among them was a reteaming with Billy Wilder for *Irma la Douce*, released in 1963 by United Artists with Shirley Maclaine in the starring role. Monroe was also mentioned as the star of a biography of Jean Harlow. In fact, on Sunday, August 5, she reportedly had made plans to meet with journalist Sidney Skolsky to discuss her role as Jean Harlow. Eventually released in 1965 by Paramount, *Harlow* would star Carroll Baker. Kim Novak would replace Monroe in 1964's *Kiss Me, Stupid,* a comedy which would have reteamed Monroe with her *Something's Got to Give* co-star, Dean Martin.

Other possible projects associated with her included a film version of the Broadway play, "A Tree Grows In Brooklyn," filmed as a musical with Frank Sinatra as her costar. On Monday, August 6, Monroe even had a date with Gene Kelly to discuss his co-starring with her in *What a Way to Go!*

In addition to the renewal of her contract with Fox for $1 million to complete *Something's Got to Give* and *What a Way to Go!*, Monroe also was reportedly negotiating with Italian filmmakers a four picture deal estimated at $10 million. The deal would give her script, director, and co-star approval and likely would keep her productive through the remainder of the 1960s.

By all accounts, Monroe had turned a corner by the late summer of 1962, and things were finally going her way. Whitey Snyder, her friend and makeup man, saw her during that last week of her life, finding her upbeat about the opportunities coming her way. She "never looked better [and] was in great spirits," he recalled.

However, Monroe knew the challenge before her was to evolve the Marilyn Monroe brand beyond the sexy, breathless creature that had made her a star and into a seasoned and capable actress that could inhabit any number of different roles. If *Something's Got to Give* had helped her enter into the role of a mature actress and mother, roles in films like *Kiss Me, Stupid; The Stripper* and *What A Way to Go!* would have to be

crafted with enough depth to allow her and her fans to see beyond the surface. Otherwise, she would have continued to fight to do a different kind of picture. It was a difficult dance at which Monroe was not always skilled.

In 1958, Truman Capote's novella *Breakfast at Tiffany's* was published by Random House and printed in a November 1958 issue of *Esquire* magazine. Its main character, Holly Golightly, was destined for the movies; and by 1960, the film version was under development by Paramount Pictures. Capote had always said the inspiration for the story's main character was Marilyn Monroe, and he wanted to see her starring in the film. Paramount hired screenwriter George Axelrod to craft the screenplay for Monroe and offered her the part.

However, as the new decade came into view, Monroe sought the advice of Lee Strasberg on how to continue to evolve herself as an actress. When Strasberg advised her that playing a prostitute would be bad for her image, she turned the part down, opting instead to film *The*

Misfits – another story with a character that had been crafted with her in mind.

Audrey Hepburn would ultimately be hired to star in *Breakfast at Tiffany's*, much to Capote's disappointment, but the film would be an immense success. Budgeted at just $2.5 million, the picture would pull in some $14 million, making it one of the biggest hits of the year and ensuring the enduring stardom of its leading lady. Hepburn would go on to be nominated for the Academy Award for Best Actress, though losing the Oscar to Sophia Loren for *Two Women*.

Declining *Breakfast at Tiffany's* could be considered one of the worst decisions Monroe would make in her career. Had she pulled off the starring role – created with her in mind – she may very well have seen a turning point in her career. An Academy Award nomination following on the heels of her Golden Globe win for *Some Like It Hot* might have taken her career to a new level. The box office success and critical acclaim might very well have put her in a position of strength in negotiating with Fox and in earning her the roles and paychecks she desired. Instead, *The Misfits*, marred by logistic and creative nightmares, would lead to the end of her marriage and an overdose that nearly took her life. *The Misfits*

would barely make what it cost, regarded both a critical and financial failure. It's only recognition came from the fact that it would mark the final screen appearances of Clark Gable and Marilyn Monroe.

In a similar twist, Doris Day's film career would be marred by an ill-conceived notion of what her onscreen persona should be. Day's success in the latter 1950s and early 1960s as America's sweetheart and the girl next door would become problematic as the actress aged into her 40s. James Garner admitted that Doris was "different than the girl-next-door" image that the public saw on the movie screen. "You can't miss with a girl like that. I'd rather have Doris than Liz Taylor. Everything Doris does turns to box office gold. And she is not the wholesome, malt-drinking, all-American girl everyone supposes."

However, Day's husband, Marty Melcher, was consumed with the idea that a wholesome Doris Day was the only persona her fans would accept. For that, her movie career would suffer. While Day would succeed as the savior to Fox with *Move Over, Darling*, and would drag out a few years more playing similar characters, the end was in sight. She would recapture the spotlight in 1964 by reteaming with Rock Hudson for Universal's *Send Me No Flowers*, and would team with Rod

Taylor for two similar pictures – first, Fox's *Do Not Disturb* in 1965, and then *The Glass Bottom Boat*, released by MGM in 1966. Melcher's Arwin Productions was behind the production of both films, as well as her turn in a wholesome western with *The Ballad of Josie* in 1967. Some called the failed western the beginning of the end of her film career, with Melcher focused on keeping Day working, so that the money would continue flowing. His financial house of cards was about to crumble.

An attempt to cast Day as the same, silly character caught up in spy tactics fizzled with the 1967 feature *Caprice*, Melcher returned her to more familiar ground with *Where Were You When the Lights Went Out?* and *With Six You Get Eggroll*, both released in 1968. By then, the world was changing and the wholesome virginal character that was the foundation of Day's onscreen persona was out of style. Independent, strong and outspoken women with modern attitudes and styles were coming into their own. She had turned down films like *The Sound of Music* and *Hello Dolly*, believing the musical was not where her future lay.

When Melcher died on April 20, 1968, Doris was shocked to find that her husband and his business partner, Jerome Bernard Rosenthal, had squandered the fortune she had earned over the previous two

decades. Leaving her deeply in debt, she filed suit against Rosenthal in February 1969, but it would take years of litigation before she would see any financial recoveries. However, Doris learned that one of Melcher's last actions on her behalf was to sign her to TV series deal with CBS. The commitment led to her starring in *The Doris Day Show* from 1968 to 1973. While the experience was far from a happy one, the series represented an income that she needed and helped her rebound from being swindled.

In 1967, when Melcher was still the driving force behind Day's career, she was approached to star in the film version of the 1963 novel, *The Graduate*. Directed by Mike Nichols, the film would be considered one of the best comedies of the decade, with Academy Award nominations for Best Picture, Best Director, Best Actor, Best Actress, Best Supporting Actress, Best Screenplay and Best Cinematography. Doris turned down the role of Mrs. Robinson, because it wasn't a fit with the onscreen persona she and Melcher has spent more than a decade building. With nudity, language and frank discussion of sex, the role would have represented a major departure for the actress. Doris Day and her husband were not willing to take that chance. Had Day taken the role of Mrs. Robinson in *The Graduate,* like Monroe's chance with *Breakfast at Tiffany's,* it might have been a major turning point in her career, taking her to a new level from which to build.

For both actresses, the roles they left behind speak as loudly about their careers as those they accepted.

Goddess & the Girl Next Door

twenty-three

"If you can make a woman laugh, you can make her do anything."
- Marilyn Monroe

-

"It's funny that so many people seem to identify closely with me or the roles I play."
- Doris Day

Closure.

Of her own death, Marilyn once remarked, "Sometimes I think it would be easier to avoid old age, to die young, but then you'd never complete your life, would you? You'd never wholly know yourself."

When Lee Strasberg died in 1982, his third wife, Anna Mizrahi Strasberg, inherited everything. A former actress, her career never amounted to much until marrying Strasberg in 1967, after Paula Strasberg's death in 1966. She had never known Marilyn Monroe, although the two had met once.

Monroe's will noted that Lee Strasberg was to inherit the majority of her belongings and to, "distribute these, in his sole discretion, among my friends, colleagues and those to whom I am devoted." However, Monroe's artifacts remained in storage for years, until Anna Strasberg assumed responsibility for the estate after his death. Everything had remained boxed and in excellent condition except for the black dress Monroe had worn when she announced her engagement to Arthur Miller, which had sadly been destroyed by moths.

In October 1999, Anna Strasberg contracted with Christie's auction house to sell the bulk of Marilyn's estate. Labeled "The Sale of The Century," the auction was held over a two-day period and earned some $13 million. On sale were nearly 576 lots of Marilyn's personal belongings. Items included her clothes, jewelry, furs and shoes, as well as furniture from her Bentwood home. Film scripts, books, awards, and even her

cosmetics brought in large sums from fans wanting a piece of one of the world's brightest stars.

The dress Marilyn wore that May evening to sing Happy Birthday to President John F. Kennedy – the event that led to her being fired from *Something's Got to Give* – sold during the auction for nearly $1.3 million. It holds the record for being the most expensive dress ever sold at auction. The white dress Marilyn wore in *The Seven Year Itch*, during the subway scene, sold for $5.6 million in 2011, holding the record for the most expensive film costume ever sold at auction.

Anna Strasberg sold more of Marilyn Monroe's estate through Julien's Auctions in June 2005. In the years since, other auctions have sold and re-sold Marilyn's personal effects. With a current estimated net worth of $27 million, Monroe remains one of the most enduring personalities Hollywood ever produced and her estate continues to rake in millions. She left a remarkable legacy, considering she never won an Academy Award and is credited with having only made 33 feature films, including her incomplete final film, *Something's Got to Give*.

The completion of *Move Over, Darling*, would mark Day's 33rd

film by 1963. While her career would include a handful more films and television work, she would recede from the limelight of Hollywood to Carmel California, not far from the shores of Monterey, where portions of *Move Over, Darling* were filmed. She fell in love with the area and settled into a quiet, private estate, dedicating her energy to a cause she held dear – the care and treatment of animals. She established the Doris Day Animal Foundation in 1978.

A life-long animal lover, Doris found that that through her own organization and celebrity status, she could make a difference in the lives of animals. She initially founded the Doris Day Pet Foundation, which focused on finding homes for animals. This would lead to her larger foundation, which helps cover spay/neuter programs, veterinary expenses, animals for seniors programs, pet food pantries, wildlife rehabilitation, educational resources and more. It became a personal cause that defined her, as much as her career in film or music.

Her films and music continued to generate interest and a healthy income until her death in 2019, with Day's net worth currently estimated at $20 million. Doris once said, "I'm tired of being thought of as Miss

Goody Two-Shoes, the girl next door, Miss Happy-Go-Lucky."

Filmsite.org ranked the 50 most successful actresses of all time. The criteria for ranking them considered factors like awards, critical acclaim for their work and the financial success of their films. Doris Day landed on the list at number 40, with Marilyn Monroe falling in just behind her at number 44. Day and Monroe fell behind other leading ladies like Bette Davis, Ingrid Bergman, Audrey Hepburn, Barbra Streisand, Katherine Hepburn and Elizabeth Taylor, but considering neither woman ever won an Academy Award for Best Actress, the feat is worthy of note. Due to their successes as box office draws – with strong and loyal fan bases – both Marilyn Monroe and Doris Day have legacies well intact that will remain for generations to come.

twenty-four

Goddess & the Girl Next Door

"A career is born in public, talent in privacy."
- Marilyn Monroe

-

"Hollywood and the networks so often say, 'We're giving the public what it wants.' But the public never really knows what it wants until somebody gives it to them."
- Doris Day

Filmography of Marilyn Monroe.

The feature films of Marilyn Monroe.

1962

Something's Got to Give (Unfinished)

Ellen Arden

1961

The Misfits
Roslyn Taber

1960

Let's Make Love
Amanda Dell

1959

Some Like It Hot
Sugar Kane Kowalczyk

1957

The Prince and the Showgirl
Elsie

1956

Bus Stop
Chérie

1955

The Seven Year Itch
The Girl

1954

There's No Business Like Show Business
Vicky Parker

River of No Return
Kay Weston

1953

How to Marry a Millionaire
Pola Debevoise

Gentlemen Prefer Blondes
Lorelei Lee

Niagara
Rose Loomis

1952

Monkey Business
Miss Lois Laurel

O. Henry's Full House
Streetwalker (segment "The Cop and the Anthem")

Don't Bother to Knock
Nell Forbes

We're Not Married!
Annabel Jones Norris

Clash by Night
Peggy

1951
Let's Make It Legal
Joyce Mannering

Love Nest
Roberta 'Bobbie' Stevens

As Young as You Feel
Harriet

Home Town Story
Iris Martin

1950

All About Eve
Miss Casswell

The Fireball
Polly

Right Cross
Dusky Ledoux (uncredited)

The Asphalt Jungle
Angela Phinlay

A Ticket to Tomahawk
Clara (uncredited)

1949

Love Happy
Grunion's Client

1948

Ladies of the Chorus
Peggy Martin

Green Grass of Wyoming
Extra at Square Dance (uncredited)

Scudda Hoo! Scudda Hay!
Betty (uncredited)

You Were Meant for Me
Undetermined Minor Role (unconfirmed, uncredited)

1947

Dangerous Years
Evie - Waitress at the Gopher Hole

twenty-five

"Sometimes I think I should have stayed longer and I should have done more films."

- Doris Day

"An actress is not a machine, but they treat you like a machine – a money machine."

- Marilyn Monroe

Filmography of Doris Day.

The feature film roles starring Doris Day.

1968
With Six You Get Eggroll

Abby McClure

Where Were You When the Lights Went Out?
Margaret Garrison
1967

Caprice
Patricia Foster

The Ballad of Josie
Josie Minick

1966

The Glass Bottom Boat
Jennifer Nelson

1965

Do Not Disturb
Janet Harper

1964

Send Me No Flowers
Judy

1963

Move Over, Darling
Ellen Wagstaff Arden

The Thrill of It All
Beverly Boyer

1962
Billy Rose's Jumbo
Kitty Wonder

That Touch of Mink
Cathy Timberlake

1961

Lover Come Back
Carol Templeton

1960

Midnight Lace
Kit Preston

Please Don't Eat the Daisies
Kate Robinson Mackay

1959

Pillow Talk
Jan Morrow

It Happened to Jane
Jane Osgood

1958

The Tunnel of Love
Isolde Poole
Teacher's Pet
Erica Stone

1957
The Pajama Game
Babe Williams

1956

Julie
Julie Benton

The Man Who Knew Too Much
Josephine Conway McKenna

1955

Love Me or Leave Me
Ruth Etting

1954

Young at Heart
Laurie Tuttle

Lucky Me
Candy Williams
1953

Calamity Jane
Calamity Jane
So You Want a Television Set (Short) (uncredited)
By the Light of the Silvery Moon
Marjorie Winfield

1952

April in Paris
Ethel S. 'Dynamite' Jackson

The Winning Team
Aimee Alexander

1951

Starlift
Doris Day

I'll See You in My Dreams
Grace LeBoy Kahn

On Moonlight Bay
Marjorie Winfield

Lullaby of Broadway
Melinda Howard

Storm Warning
Lucy Rice

1950

The West Point Story
Jan Wilson
 Tea for Two
Nanette Carter

Young Man with a Horn
Jo Jordan

1949

It's a Great Feeling
Judy Adams

My Dream Is Yours
Martha Gibson

1948

Romance on the High Seas
Georgia Garrett

Appendix

sources

Selected Bibliography.

A number of books, magazines, newspapers, documentaries and interviews, as well as the films themselves provided sources of information and factual data that went into the writing of this book. Thank you to the many sources referenced throughout the book. There were many individuals whose work, insights, reviews, comments and suggestions that also helped make this book possible.

Books

Bego, Mark. "Rock Hudson: Public and Private." 1986. Signet. New York.

Braun, Eric. "Doris Day." 1991. Orion Books. London.

Brodsky, Jack and Weiss, Nathan. "The Cleopatra Papers." 1963. Simon and Schuster. New York.

Brown, Peter Harry and Barham, Patte B. "Marilyn: The Last Take." 1992. Dutton Books. New York.

Finler, Joel W. "The Hollywood Story." 1988. Crown Publishers, Inc. New York.

Garner, James and Winokur, John. "The Garner Files." 2011. Simon & Schuster. New York.

Hingham, Charles. "Audrey - The Life of Audrey Hepburn." 1984. Macmillan Publishing Company. New York.

Hirschhorn, Clive. "The Universal Story." 1983. Crown Publishers, Inc. New York.

Kaufman, David. "Doris Day: The Untold Story of the Girl Next Door." 2008. Virgin Books. New York.

Levy, Emanuel. "George Cukor: Master of Elegance." 1994. William Morrow and Company. New York.

Madsen, Axel. "John Huston." 1978. Doubleday & Company. New York.

McGilligan, Patrick. "George Cukor: A Double Life." 2013. University of Minnesota Press. Minneapolis.

Murray, Eunice. "Marilyn: The Last Months." 1975. Pyramid Books. New York.

Nelson, Nancy. "Evenings with Cary Grant." 1991. Warner Books. New York.

Smith, Matthew. "Marilyn's Last Words." 2004. Carroll & Graf. New York.

Spada, James. "Peter Lawford: The Man Who Kept the Secrets." 1991. Bantam Books. New York.

Spada, James. "Monroe." 1982. Dolphin Books. New York.

Stallings, Penny. "Flesh and Fantasy." 1978. New York. St. Martin's Press.

Strasberg, Susan. "Marilyn and Me." 1992. Warner Books.

Summers, Anthony. "Goddess." 1985. New York. McMillan Publishing.

Walker, Alexander. "Elizabeth." 1990. New York. Grove Weidenfeld.

Williams, Gregory Paul. "The Story of Hollywood." 2005. BL Press LLC. Los Angeles.

Willis, David and Schmidt, Stephen. "Marilyn Monroe: Metamorphosis." 2011. Harper Collins. New York.

Print Periodicals, Newspapers and Magazines

Bigsby, Christopher. "Marilyn Monroe and Arthur Miller: extract from Christopher Bigsby's biography." The Telegraph. November 16, 2008.

Bret, David. "The dark days of Doris Day: The 'girl next door' had a dark side behind her squeaky clean public image." The Daily Mail. June 25, 2008.

Bret, David. "How Doris Day's third husband cost her sanity - and her £66million fortune." The Daily Mail. June 15, 2008.

Carlisle, Candice. "The former Cabana Motor Hotel is under contract (again) but this time to a hotel developer." Dallas Business Journal. November 9, 2016.

Crowther, Bosley. "Screen: John Huston's 'The Misfits.' The New York Times. February 2, 1961.

Crowther, Bosley. "Screen: 'The Thrill of It All' Opens at Music Hall: Doris Day Stars in Carl Reiner Comedy." The New York Times. August 2, 1963.

Crowther, Bosley. "Screen: Eight New Movies Arrive for the Holidays:Natalie Wood Starred as a Salesgirl Doris Day Is in 'Move Over, Darling' 'Move Over, Darling' 'Sleeping in My Bed' 'The Best of Cinerama' 'Sword in the Stone' '4 for Texas' of 1870 'Kings of the Sun' '30 Years of Fun'." The. New York Times. December 26, 1963.

David, Mark. "Marilyn Monroe Died Here." Variety. July 14, 2010.

Drew, Bernard. "John Huston – At 74 No Formulas." American Film. September 1980.

Hopper, Hedda. "Doris Day, Melcher After South Pacific." Los Angeles Times. May 14, 1956.

Kaufman, David. "Doris Day's Vanishing Act." Vanity Fair. May 1, 2008.

McConnell, Jim. "Pearson definitely stood tall." The Sun Sports. February 7, 2012

McLellan, Dennis. "Film producer David Brown ('Jaws,' 'Cocoon') has died." Washington Post. February 3, 2010.

Molotsky, Irwin. "F.B.I. Releases Its Sinatra File, With Tidbits Old and New." The New York Times. December 9, 1998.

Nessif, Bruna. "Marilyn Monroe's Medical Records and X-Rays Confirm Plastic Surgery—Take a Look!" E!News. October 10, 2013.

O'hara, Helen. "How Marilyn Took on Hollywood – and Won." The Telegraph. June 1, 2015.

Staff. "Review: 'Thrill of It All.'" Variety. December 31, 1962

Staff. "Review: 'Move Over Darling.'" Variety. December 31, 1962.

Tonguette, Peter. "Fifth Avenue, 5 AM: Audrey Hepburn, Breakfast at Tiffany's, and the Dawn of the Modern Woman." Cineaste. 2010.

Internet Sources

Eder, Bruce. "Joe Lubin." Allmusic.com. 2016

Kniestedt, Kevin. "How Marilyn Monroe changed Ella Fitzgerald's life. KNKX. March 22, 2012.

Hanks, Tara. "Patricia Newcomb." Immortal Marilyn. 2015.

Levy, Emanuel. "Marilyn Monroe's Last Role; Cukor Talks about his Star." Cinema 24/7. January 16, 2006.

Samuel, Patrick. "A Tale of Two Wives." StaticMass.net. March 18, 2011.

Additional Internet sources to cross-checking and comparison.

Wikipedia: www.wikipedia.com

The Internet Movie Database: www.imdb.com

The Numbers – Box Office Data, Movie Stars, Idle Speculation: www.the-numbers.com

Box Office Mojo: www.boxofficemojo.com

The Marilyn Monroe Collection: http://themarilynmonroecollection.com

Photo Credits

In addition to the selected bibliography of sources we would also like to acknowledge the many photographs used in this book. While some are part of the author's private collection, we would like to specifically acknowledge the following for illustrations used that are used for the purpose of review to highlight and complement the text:

MGM; Twentieth Century Fox; United Artists, Universal; Paramount Pictures, Sipa Press; Life Magazine; The LA Times; NY Daily News and CBS Records. Contact the publisher at editorial@aplombpublishing.com if you have questions.

Goddess & the Girl Next Door

index

Index

About the Author

J ohn William Law is a writer and journalist whose work has appeared in newspapers, magazines and books. He has worked on the staffs of daily, weekly and monthly publications. He is the author of numerous books and narrates a podcast on iTunes entitled *Behind the Screen with The Movie Files*. He has appeared on television and film documentaries discussing film history and on national public radio. His 2010 book, *Alfred Hitchcock: The Icon Years* was named Best Non-Fiction title in the Readers Favorite Book Awards and in 2014 his book *Who Nuked The Duke?* was named Best Non-Fiction title in the San Francisco Book Festival. In 2016, his book *Movie Star & the Mobster* won the London, New York and Hollywood Book Festivals for Best General Non-Fiction. He lives in San Francisco. His books include:

Curse of the Silver Screen - Tragedy & Disaster Behind the Movies (1999, Aplomb Publishing)

Scare Tactic - The Life and Films of William Castle (2000, Writers Club Press)

Reel Horror - True Horrors Behind Hollywood's Scary Movies (2004, Aplomb Publishing)

Master of Disaster: Irwin Allen - The Disaster Years (2008, Aplomb Publishing)

Alfred Hitchcock: The Icon Years (2010, Aplomb Publishing)

What Ever Happened to Mommie Dearest? (2012, Aplomb Publishing)

Who Nuked the Duke? (2014, Aplomb Publishing)

Movie Star & the Mobster (2016, Aplomb Publishing)

The Lost Hitchcocks (2018, Aplomb Publishing)